The
GIFTS
of the
SPIRIT

FOR A NEW GENERATION

DR· KERRY WOOD

Cover Design: Ivethe Zambrano-Fernández
wwwdesignbytwo.com

Layout Design by Burkhart Books
www.BurkhartBooks.com

Cover graphic: Freepik.com

www.zadoksupply.com

Endorsements

The passionate pursuit of the workings of God by His Spirit can only be a pursuit for God Himself. Our God is an overflowing fountain of compassion pouring forth in such measure as to be mistaken for raw power. This fullness of compassion, given as gifts to advance His divine purposes in us and to the world, is not found at new and exotic places. These gifts are where they have always been, "All my springs are in You" (Ps. 87:7). "Deep calls unto deep at the noise of Your waterfalls" (Ps. 42:7). But these must be rediscovered by every generation.

The Gifts of the Spirit for a New Generation is no call to submerge the human psyche in mystical Christianity, but a practical focus toward the fulfillment of His *telos* (purpose) upon the lives of a generation that must see the demonstration of the Spirit's power in a way that few generations have seen. These are critical days.

C. S. Lewis observed the human temptation to intellectualize vanity, and emptiness issuing from any pursuit of the mind that is unaccompanied by the nurture of the spirit. In many ways he described the current generation well as "people without chests, whose hearts have atrophied." Ours, both inside the church and out, is a culture that perceives itself as technologically advanced, even as it continues to shrivel within for want of spiritual substance. These are not days in which the Church can afford to minimize the conversation about, nor carelessly disregard, the life of the Spirit.

Happily, Kerry Wood, a seasoned pastor, student and friend, is not averse to dealing with the necessities of the Spirit in soundly biblical, passionately spiritual and abundantly practical ways. I recommend him to you.

—*Jack Hayford*
Pastor, Author,
Founder, The Church on the Way (Van Nuys, CA)
Founder and Chancellor, The King's University

This is Kerry's first published book but it will certainly not be his last. Kerry is one of a new generation of writers who have pressed through to understand what made the difference to the generation of the 50-60's and beyond. It was the working of the Holy Spirit that took frail humanity empowered by that same Spirit and changed the face of Christendom. Kerry lives what he writes and has a passion to see a new generation empowered by the Spirit to accomplish God's purposes on the earth and see the Kingdom come. Walk with this man in his highs and lows, share his longing, and discover his total dependence on the Holy Spirit which is the only means that God has given us to reach this lost generation. Read and be inspired to seek so that a new day may dawn for those who claim to be His disciples.

—*Norman Barnes*
Founder, Links International

Gifts of the Spirit is a journey with a master sailor who has been out to sea and now wants to invite others to come along. Life in the Spirit is a vivid biblical concept that needs to be revitalized for the future life of the church and the world. Dr. Kerry Wood brings the passion of his own personal life transformation to ignite a younger generation to catch the wind that fills our sails to go on an adventure with the living God. This is lived from the gifts of the grace-filled God who desires to bless the world through willing and connected servants. Hoist the sail and dive in!

—*Marty Folsom, PhD*
Author, Face to Face book series
Executive Director, Pacific Association for Theological Studies.

One of the ills of our civilization is to focus more on doing than on being, and that has had a profound effect upon Christianity. Redemption was intended to restore the image and likeness that was broken in the Garden of Eden – in other words, to restore our identity and our relationship with our heavenly Father. How refreshing it is to find this book, which is focused on being, with the depth and simplicity that are characteristic of Dr. Wood.

The great protagonist of the Church era is the Holy Spirit—but going beyond theological knowledge or ecstatic experience, do we really have a relationship with Him?

Pastor Kerry's life and ministry have challenged us to move forward in a relationship with the Holy Spirit, to have a continual walk in the supernatural, and to overcome the orphan spirit to which the Church has succumbed. The relationship with the Holy Spirit is God's plan for everyone, not just for a few privileged ones (as some have led us to believe), a life that it is lived out of "being before doing".

This book is for those who want to "be" in order to "do."

—*Andrés Vargas*
Senior Pastor, El Río Christian Church
Bogotá, Colombia

Eugene Peterson says, 'This world is no friend to grace.'

We are driven by achievement, recognition of talent above character, making icons of cult personalities, self- centeredness. We have a need to be in control.

The work of the Spirit is all about Grace. Gifts that are not earned, though truly earnestly sought.

Kerry Wood is a man of the Spirit. Essentially therefore, a man of the Word. He understands, not merely from an academic perspective but as a lifestyle necessity, that it's only by grace that we receive God's fragrant gifts.

I commend Kerry as a worshipper, one 'who stands in the presence of the Lord'. These writings have come from that Throne room experience.

—*Rev Canon Chris Bowater OSL*
Founder, Worship Academy International
Senior Pastor, New Life Church Ministries, Sleaford, England

For a few years my son, who studied under Kerry, would say, "Dad, you wouldn't believe what Kerry Wood said today!" And it was always interesting and relevant. So I read this book with an expectation that was not disappointed. This book has some great paradoxes:

It is a practical book, but not a "how to" book. Kerry does not tell us how to point the hose. He just tells how to jump in the stream.

This is not some guy yelling at us to get back to the old days, but an astonished man calling us to the new day where the gifts are flowing. They may not be flowing in the mainstream church, but they are flowing in the mainstream of God's compassion.

Kerry writes with the clarity of a professor, but like a prophet, he invites us into the land where understanding can't keep pace.

Finally, this book gets us excited about the gifts, but more so with the love-crazed Giver.

This is a must book for the generation tired of cocky preachers manipulating the gifts of the Spirit like a gunslinger blowing the smoke off the gun barrel. How refreshing to see Kerry with the smoking gun and big round eyes, saying, "Wow".

Moving in the gifts is not weird or religious, but it is scary, wonderful and astonishing.

—*Pastor Andrew McMillan*
Comunidad Cristiana de Fe, Medellin, Colombia

I am so pleased to have the privilege to endorse Kerry Wood and his new book "Gifts of the Spirit for a New Generation." I have, on many occasions, sat with Kerry as the Spirit has used him to speak deep truth from the heart of God into my life. His desire to see the people intimately walk as sons and daughters with Father God is so overwhelming that you cannot help but leave the conversation wanting more of the gifts of the Spirit in your own life. His insight into the gifts of the Spirit will both encourage and challenge you to run hard towards the heart of God as well. Enjoy your journey into "Gifts of the Spirit for a New Generation." You will never be the same.

—*Tony Shupp*
Lead Pastor, CityLife Church, Bedford, Texas

DEDICATION

This book is dedicated to my godly parents,

Max and Mary Wood,

who faithfully and constantly made the tough decisions
necessary to keep their children in a church where
the presence and reality of the Spirit was the priority.

And to my grandmother, **Flora Massey,**
who may not have been able to expound upon
the gifts of the Spirit eloquently,
but lived in the overflow fullness of them,
introducing everyone she knew to "the Comforter",
until her last days just shy of her 106th birthday.

Acknowledgments

Since I hold to the Hebraic view of personhood, that a person is the culmination of all those of his family lineage and those who have impacted his life, acknowledgements can't be an easy thing. Even God calls Himself by those to whom He relates (e.g., the God of Abraham, Isaac and Jacob). So how does one adequately acknowledge those who have contributed to his work, which is a by-product of who he is?

I don't suspect that I am even fully aware of all who have contributed to my life and where I am, but I am thankful for the Lord's masterful ability to make my life a tapestry, and for every person He has used to encourage and invest in me along the way. But a few must be articulated more clearly.

First, my brilliant and beautiful wife, Chiqui, who has walked with me through every step of the creative process, giving great insights, asking questions, even challenging my thinking on things I've asserted. In every step she has made this little book better than it would have been. This is how we work together and we love it. In addition, and a large one at that, she translated this work into Spanish.

I am grateful to my parents, Max and Mary Wood, for bringing me up in a home that always placed the priority on finding and doing the will of God, whatever that might be, and pursuing the Presence of God at all costs. I hope you have caught that rich heritage and my appreciation for my dear parents in these pages.

To too many spiritual mentors to mention, but Jack Hayford has had a profound impact upon me. Thank you, Pastor Jack.

I am grateful to Tod Williams at Zadok Publishing for his friendship and for believing deeply in this project. And finally, to Tim Taylor at Burkhart Books, for his experience, wisdom and counsel.

I am blessed and grateful with such a rich treasure of friendships far and wide.

CONTENTS

PREFACE

A Call to a New Spiritual Generation

The New Testament is filled with the evidence that God never intended to confine the outpouring of the Spirit to one historic day.

—B.H. Clendennen

Perhaps you only want to read about the gifts of the Spirit from a mighty miracle-worker, someone known for filling stadiums and convention centers. Perhaps you only want to read a book on the gifts by someone who has stories to tell about all nine gifts of the Spirit, someone who has wrestled with angels and demons alike, and who can tell you your name, address and phone number by word of knowledge at the drop of a hat. That's understandable. However, if that's the case, you may not want to read any further. I wear no cape, no blue undershirt with a big red superman 'S' on it. I've been around miracles and healings almost all my life and have no trouble saying I feel comfortable around God moving in ways that may seem weird to some, but I am just like you. I have good days and bad days. In fact, I've had good years and bad years!

A few decades of pastoral ministry and a handful of years as adjunct professor have taught me that we are all on a journey together. No one has it all figured out—but we must remain diligent learners. One of the things I have learned is that we all have a deep hunger for more than we are currently experiencing, even if that hunger is muted by distractions or nearer-to-the-surface passions. We are spirit beings made for spiritual adventure. What I have also learned is that entire generations, both spiritual and natural, can get disenchanted, disenfranchised and disengaged about the things of the Spirit, and spend their lives taking up other causes, or the cause of not believing in causes. This book is about re-awakening a hunger, from one sojourner to another; about one learner sharing some experiences to provoke other learners to get their own. Quite simply, *I believe there is a correlation between the Church's lack of effectiveness and her inattentiveness to the gifts that the Father, Son, and Spirit have provided her to accomplish the mission.*

This is a call from one generation to another. To be clear, when speaking of a generation as a spiritual movement or the life of the Church in its current state, we cannot think only in terms of a chronological or biological generation. When I speak of "a call to a new generation," I am not referring only to the Builders, Busters, Boomers, Gen-Xers, Millennials or whatever sociological tag comes after that. Though this may be applicable to a specific age-group, we must also consider that the Church is in different stages of spiritual maturity depending on the continent or even the movement to which one happens to be referring. Though most of my experience is in the North American Church, even a spiritual generation here is a complicated issue and generalizations are just that, and never totally accurate. With that being said, a new generation needs to hear a call to the gifts that are constantly flowing from our infinite overflowing, other-centered God. Who will offer these gifts, these rivers of revelation, utterance and power, as manifestations of God's compassion to a broken world?

Peter Krause said, "Parenthood... is about guiding the next generation, and forgiving the last." I am afraid that the next generation of spiritual leaders, if they find their way to the compassion of God that is released through the demonstration of the Spirit's power, will have to do a lot of forgiving of my spiritual generation.

My intent is not to point fingers—except to point out issues. It is my generation (and that is a generalization) that has failed to model a rich and powerful heritage in the things of the Spirit for the generations to follow. I would not have understood this so clearly except for the exposure I have had to the next generation as a pastor and professor. Serving in a Bible College/Seminary setting these past few years, one that is filled with young men and women full of zeal to follow the Lord, I have become aware of a growing chasm between my childhood experiences in church and those to which these emerging leaders have been exposed. When I mentioned giants in the faith that have impacted my life so profoundly—leaders like Smith Wigglesworth, John G. Lake,

F.F. Bosworth, Aimee Semple McPherson, Kathryn Kuhlman, T.L. Osborn or Oral Roberts—I was met with blank stares. To my amazement, most of these students had never heard of these pioneers of the faith

As I probed deeper, I discovered many had never heard about spiritual language (speaking in tongues as prayer language) as a daily discipline. And many had never received Spirit Baptism for themselves.

THE APPS GENERATION

There is something both glorious and deadly about the surge of technological advancement that my generation and my parents' generation have witnessed. It would be fun to elaborate many of the changes we have seen in the last twenty or thirty years alone, but others can and have done it better, and of course, that information can be Googled instantly.

One huge difference between my generation and my kids' generation—they have never known anything but Apple, iPods, iPhones and the internet. My generation stays in conflict about the dizzying pace at which new models of everything techno is being developed. Social media has forever changed the world's patterns of personal interaction. It is not cool to be behind the curve on the latest app that has "come out." Think about that; the social pressure that is on everyone to stay up with the latest and fastest is enormous. The latest car commercial announces that even grandma can be somewhat cool if she has a blog.

Why is this significant? Is there anything wrong with everyone being so driven by the mindset that "this is where everything is going"? We hear it constantly at the job: "If you are not up on technology you won't get hired...." "This is where everything is going" (i.e. all technology and internet driven)...." "In five years we won't be doing it this way anymore...."

Will internet church replace geographically local church? Will there come a time when people don't "go to church" anymore—just download "church" instead? What about personal ministry? Will the church app replace the need or experience to gather for prayer, to have hands laid on the sick, or to be anointed with oil? What does this mean for the scriptural admonitions to "not forsake the assembling of yourselves together," or to "call for the elders of the church to anoint with oil and pray the prayer of faith for the sick," or to abound in the fellowship (*koinonia*) of the Holy Spirit? How are the gifts to be manifest for the edification, exhortation and comfort of the Body of Christ if we are not together? Yes, we could email a prophecy, but can we "know those that labor among you" well enough to do that in a spiritually safe way? And what keeps any person, whether called, proven, prepared or not from appointing themselves as pastor or prophet and setting up a non-accountable online church?

These questions are not intended to discourage but to open a dialogue with God about where this is all going in the light of His kingdom purposes of "Binding up the bruised, setting at liberty the captive and giving sight to the blind." Invariably it brings us back to the question, "Do we still need the Gifts?"

PART I - FOUNDATION

THE IMPORTANCE OF THE GIFTS OF THE SPIRIT

In a life of participation in God's Kingdom rule, we are not to make things happen, but to be honestly willing and eager to be made able.

—Dallas Willard

Vinson Synan, a researcher and student of trends within Christian movements (especially Pentecostal and Charismatic), characterized the Twentieth Century as "the Century of the Holy Spirit." The explosive opening of that century with outpourings of the Spirit all over the world, perhaps most notably the Azusa Street Revival in Los Angeles, did not abate throughout the 1900s. The closer we came to the end of that century it seemed the revivals were beginning to catch up and overtake one another. The large tent healing revivals of the 1940s and 50s in North America became the Latter Rain prophetic movement, which was eclipsed by the Word of Faith movement, then eclipsed by the Charismatic movement and a surge of fresh worship that swept many nations and seemed to be culminating in a grand finale of joy in the 90s. It seemed as though the birth pangs of the Spirit were getting closer and closer, so to speak, and the culmination and conclusion of the Church Age was imminent. Then, at the end of the century, a strange malaise set in.

Concurrent with numerous spiritual outpourings was also a simultaneous social rise in godless humanism and explosions in technology. Not being a social scientist, the connections of these parallels between the spiritual dynamic and the social one, seemingly headed in opposite directions, is not one that can be easily articulated, nor is it the purpose of this book. It doesn't take a genius to see the connection between the Church's dependence upon technology (as the best that man can produce) and the lack of dependence upon Holy Spirit for supernatural ministry. Perhaps it's a bridge too far for some, but it brings me to the purpose of this book.

The first reason I feel compelled to offer this brief work now is that it seems evident that the gifts of the Spirit have taken a back seat in the 21st Century.

I understand that for many who did not grow up attending church, and many others who grew up in churches where the Holy Spirit was not a topic of discussion (much less an acceptable way of "doing church"), this sounds like a strange statement. For those that are just now coming into the things of the Spirit, all things are wonderfully new. The things of the Spirit are the new "front and center" for a few, and the idea that the Church is in some form of retreat seems preposterous. But the reality, primarily in the West, is that even where Spirit Baptism has been championed in the past, it is largely a "fundamental truth" now with a load of sentiment attached to it. The truth is articulated regularly enough, perhaps, but only practiced rarely. At the turn of Twenty-First century statistics from the largest Pentecostal denomination in the world revealed that fewer than fifty percent of its constituents claim a Spirit Baptism experience and even fewer experience manifestations of the gifts of the Spirit in their gatherings. This would have caused a rending of garments only two or three decades prior. In some ways it seems that those who fought so bravely to convince the Church that the gifts of the Spirit are necessary, are now living as if they are not. Questions need to be asked about this tragic trend.

The second reason to write this book now is that the gifts

of the Spirit have not been understood as the compassion of God—an infinite overflow of His very nature and being. I grew up in Pentecost, practically a direct line, albeit imperfectly drawn, from the Azusa Street revival. The Assemblies of God and other Pentecostal movements became champions of the Baptism in the Spirit experience and the regular operation of His gifts. In a time where Pentecost was marginalized by the denominations

If the gifts are a by-product of His unchanging nature (rather than His capricious occasional outpouring), then He cannot not give gifts!

and considered the domain of the poor and uneducated, Exile theology was helpful (though we wouldn't have known to call it such at the time). Exile Theology is grounded in the framework of slaves ever-coming out of Egypt and wandering in the wilderness, but never quite finding the Promised Land. Think of it this way—if you are poor, have little standing in the religious or social community, you are going to feel powerless. And what do powerless people need? Either a quick escape or a new form of power. For a rapidly growing wave of people in the world, Pentecost (the experience and theology) provided an immediate access to supernatural power by the gifts of the Spirit, and if need-be, an anticipated imminent escape (the rapture of the Church). And, of course, Jesus is the one who said, "You will be endued with power from on high" (I have to use the King James term 'endued' because that is what we grew up hearing and it still feels right).

I am in no way seeking to negate that the gifts of the Spirit, indeed any partnership with Holy Spirit at any level, will be a serious upgrade of power, both in the authority (*exousia*) in which it is exercised and the sheer force (*dunamis*) that is made available to believers who partner with God. But we have not generally thought of the gifts of the Spirit as an overflow of God's infinite, other-centered love and compassion. We have not thought of the gifts of the godhead (the gifts of the Father [Romans 12], the gifts of the Son [Ephesians 4] or the gifts of the

God anointed Jesus with the power of the Holy Spirit to release compassion. Spirit [1 Corinthians 12]) as a natural overflow of who God is. This is extremely significant theologically because if the gifts are a by-product of His unchanging nature (rather than His capricious occasional outpouring), then He *cannot not* give gifts! Without this theological foundation, we are drawn into feeble arguments about whether or not the gifts of the Spirit "have passed away." Let me say it this way: If His gifts are a result of God's occasional feeling of benevolence, then they are seasonal, sporadic, and optional. And if they are occasional and optional then Christians can excuse powerlessness by saying "I guess that gift is for some, but not for me." But, if the gifts of God are a result of His unchanging nature, He is always giving them and they are for everyone who will receive them.

I am convinced that the Church needs to see the gifts of the Spirit as God's divine love overflowing to the whole world, through the Church, in a compassion that longs to see the broken healed, the imprisoned set free, and the blind given sight. Jesus, the express image and exact representation of the Father, modeled this for us declaring that the Spirit of the Lord was anointing Him to do just that (Isaiah 61:1; Luke 4:18). Luke tells us that God anointed Jesus with the power of the Holy Spirit to release compassion. Grab this idea: *power to release compassion.* Jesus went about doing good, healing all that were sick and oppressed of the devil for God was with Him by the fullness of the Spirit (Acts 10:38). We have focused on the power, but perhaps the Father's compassion is the motivating force (because it's His nature); the power is simply the vehicle. I believe it is time for the Church to reclaim her place as the world's distributor of compassion, with power.

Thirdly, I believe this book is important now because the gifts of the Spirit are still being ignored. Paul said, *"Now about the gifts of the Spirit, brothers and sisters, I do not want you to be uninformed"* (1 Corinthians 12:1, NIV). The old King James says, "I would not have you be ignorant." To be ignorant is not only to be uneducated, but to ignore available information. For many in the Church, the ignorance is simply due to a lack of exposure to the truth. And for many that lack of exposure is because church leaders ignore the supernatural equipment that is available. This is all the more grievous when we consider that we live after the contemporary outpourings of the Spirit—not before them— and have ready access to information about them. We have no excuse for ignorance.

Ed Stetzer says, "American evangelicalism must learn how to engage culture from the edges instead of the center." It's strikingly close to correct, but the fact is that to engage at the edges one must be connected to the center. This is how God does what God does. It's how He is who He is. He is the outward-flowing, other-centered Being who is the center of all things—and at the same time is pressing out the edges to further points unknown—much like our created universe. The reality is the Church must engage the edges from the Center, and that is what the Church did by the Spirit in the Azusa Street revival and Charismatic movement and so many other outpourings of the Spirit. But we were too orphaned in our thinking to understanding the power of it.

What I know is that in times of stress the orphan spirit always looks for comfort. Our Western disease, both inside the Church and out, is still consumerism and comfort. And though neither consumerism nor comfort is all bad, when applied to a spiritual state it's not good. The consumerist idea is that bigger is automatically better (making "bigger" the goal). When technology is harnessed as the means to that end, we are easily deceived to believe that we have achieved real spiritual atmosphere (a fabricated form of the "presence of God") which minimizes the importance of the gifts of the Spirit in the life of a church.[1] Ultimately, though we can create church experiences with great sound, lighting and enthusiastic worship (and in some ways fabricate the glory of God), we cannot heal the brokenhearted, give sight to the blind or set the captive free with technology alone. And though I don't know of anyone who would suggest that we can, I'm not sure the next generation will be able to tell the difference, unless they see the genuine.

Finally, I am writing this book because there is a new generation that is looking for the authentic—the real deal—and the new generation is leaving the Church in droves because they are seeing a commercialized, sanitized, anemic version of Christianity that is comfortable but requires no real commitment and produces no real transformation.

Consider this open letter from a "Millennial" who is trying to explain why the Church is losing so many young people:[2]

I've always been in church. I've never left, though I've come close several times. I would have left in high school if I'd had the option, but in my house, attendance at my cool, hip, contemporary-worshiping, youth-group-glorifying, moralism-preaching, theology-eschewing McCongregation was a non-negotiable.

So I went. Through every repetition of "Shout to the Lord," every True Love Waits commitment ceremony, every rapture-ready dispensationalist Bible study, every sermon series on how to make myself into a good, moral, well-behaved person so that I wouldn't tick off God and bring condemnation to America.

But I was always a misfit. Always a skeptic. Always a doubter. Always an outsider.

The truth is, my relationship with you is still love-hate.

I love the theology, but I hate the expectations of pseudo piety.

Love the gospel, hate the patriotic moralism.

Love the Bible, hate the way it's used.

Love Jesus, but hate what we've done with him.

Love worship, but hate Jesusy entertainment.

And those other kids I went to church with, I've come to find that many of them were misfits, skeptics, and doubters, too. Some of them still go, but more of them have left.

Some of them left because they had no desire to

conform to an outdated cultural norm that demanded we keep up appearances by parking our butts in our regular Sunday pew.

They didn't believe, and didn't believe they needed to pretend that they did.

Others have left because they grew keen to the bait-and-switch tactics. They've left because they didn't fit in, and couldn't pretend anymore. They left because the Jesus preached from the pulpit didn't look much like the Jesus of Nazareth. They left because all the bells and whistles and hooks and marketing rang hollow.

Of course you notice how disappointed this representative of the Millennials sounds –even cynical. But did you notice that there is no mention of the gifts of the Spirit or the supernatural? There is a reference to "the gospel preached from the pulpit doesn't look like the Gospel Jesus preached" but it is primarily a reference to a gospel of love and inclusion versus judgment and intolerance. The gospel of power (healings and miracles) that was the vehicle of the love of Jesus, to make that which was broken whole, has been sidelined as an optional extra.

It is a work of the Spirit in this new generation to reject the judgmentalism, conformity and politicizing of the gospel. It is a work of the Spirit to be loving and accepting of all people, whether they be of diverse race, creed or sexual orientation. But God's love doesn't just say "be warmed and filled," or "feel OK about where you are and who you are." Go back and study Jesus' life again—in the gospels. God's love is communicated in a kingdom power that says "I love you too much to leave you in the mess you are in." He touches people with a power to heal what is broken. And it is my conviction that this new generation is better positioned—socially and theologically—to get the balance right. The Good News is not just that you are loved, but loved to wholeness. God, in His infinite love and compassion, wants you whole.

I am a sojourner just as you—my hindsight is better than my

foresight. But being older now, I have much more hindsight than I used to. I hope it will be helpful to a younger generation that may not have seen what I have seen. I am compelled to blow a trumpet in the Church's hearing that the gifts of the Spirit are a primary way in which God pours out His compassion on the broken. I am compelled to say this is not a time for the Holy Spirit to be limited in His free operation among men—the gifts of the Spirit cannot take a backseat now when a generation that understands the failed promises of science is hungry again for true spirituality. And I am compelled to say that there is still so much a new generation (and older alike) needs to learn about how God wants to heal the sick, bind up the wounded and set the captive free—and He is looking for partners.

DISCUSSION QUESTIONS

1. Why does the author believe that God's other-centered nature is so significant to the gifts of the Spirit?

2. What stands out to you about what the young "millennial" says about the church? Do you agree?

3. What are your expectations—your hopes or concerns—about the rest of this book?

CHAPTER ONE

GIFTS OF THE SPIRIT AS GOD'S COMPASSION

The gospel portrait of the beloved Child of Abba is that of a man exquisitely attuned to His emotions and uninhibited in expressing them.

—Brennan Manning

Growing up in a Pentecostal church I heard many messages on the importance of the Holy Spirit and the gifts of the Spirit. Experiencing the manifestations of the Spirit was not strange or weird to me. We expected the Holy Spirit to meet us when we gathered. We prayed earnestly before every service asking God to move in our gathering. We didn't know to call it by a name then, but now we call it a Presence-driven ministry. The church my family attended in my elementary school years was certainly a Presence-driven church, and I'm so grateful for it now. I cannot count the number of sermons I heard on Moses' pleading with God, *"If Your Presence does not go with us, do not bring us up from here"* (Exodus 33:15).

But we also heard a lot of preaching on "living right," "pleasing God" and being convicted of our sins. These two themes seemed to go hand-in-hand—(1) the Holy Spirit is given to convict us of our sins, and (2) He gives us power to witness and do powerful things in the Lord's name. I did not realize at the time that this combination would eventually render the Church powerless, not powerful. I would become more conscious of my sin and sinfulness than of His gifts of grace given out of His pure compassion for the breaker and the broken, the violent and the violated.

You may be tempted at this point to skip this chapter and get to the "meat." You want to know more about the gifts, the hindrances to the gifts, and how to cultivate them. But let me urge you to stay with me!

My father established a family tradition that we followed every Christmas morning. I followed the same tradition with my children, and trust they will do the same with theirs. Dad always had a pattern of sitting the family around the Christmas tree and opening his Bible to Luke 2. Of course we, as children, were anxious to get to the gifts, but we knew there was no budging on this tradition. Dad would always read the Christmas story of the birth of the Christ-child and underscore, year after year, why we were receiving these gifts. Christmas was not about the gifts, but about the Person that we celebrated by the gifts, and the overflowing love of the Father to send His only Son to us.

These gifts are no different. If we focus on the gifts and miss the Person who gives them, and His motivation for giving them, we miss that which is most important. So we must start with who God is. Please let me explain, because this will change everything about the why and how of the gifts of the Spirit. You see, what we believe about God determines what we will believe about everything else; literally everything else, including the gifts of the Spirit. Let me give you a few examples. Of course these are not all the options, and each one of these has different nuances, so please don't hear me as saying that this is the way it is, categorically. I am using these to illustrate how our view of God will affect our view of spiritual gifts, and show the importance of starting this study on the gifts with looking first at who God is. The question is, what is your view of God and how is that affecting your understanding of the gifts of the Spirit?

GOD AS LAW-GIVER AND JUDGE

If I believe God is a strict **by-the-rulebook Law-giver and Judge**, then I will also believe that He is more concerned about me being right and doing right. In this view right conduct is the most important thing; even more important than right relationships. Having my sins washed away is the most important thing because (our minds rationalize) God cannot stand to be in the presence of sin. Evidently God must avoid sin "like the plague", which means He cannot bear to be with those tainted by sin. This also shapes our view of "holiness." Holiness, in what theologians call the "judicial satisfaction view of the atonement," is keeping a distance from anything sinful or unholy. Therefore we have to keep a distance from it because it is more powerful than we are and will get on us and pollute us. So Jesus covers us with His blood so the Father can receive us in spite of our blemishes. In this view, Jesus' primary purpose for coming to the earth was to keep this angry God away from totally wretched sinners.

Stick with me here because this is going to shift your mental paradigm. I am not saying that there is no distinction between right and wrong. There is. I am not saying that we don't need forgiveness for our sins. We do, and I am eternally grateful for God's gift of salvation. But if our view of God is an angry Old Testament Law-giver and Judge, it preconditions us concerning how we live out our Christian life and about the purpose of the gifts of the Spirit.

If, as some would assert, God is all about being right, holiness is about doing the right things, and Jesus' reason for coming was to appease the angry God—to keep Him from smiting us, then the role of the Holy Spirit is to convict us (point out) our sin. Now the burden is on us to make the right decisions and get rid of the sin. Now that we have the Bible, all that we need to do is derive cause-and-effect principles and live accordingly. Our role as the Church, we deduce, is to set up an ethical and moral code that is pleasing to God. In this scenario the gifts of the Spirit were only given to the early Church until the updated rule-book (the New

Testament) was completed. Now that we have the Bible (Old and New Testaments) spiritual gifts are no longer needed.

But notice that when Jesus became flesh among us He declared that "all authority" had been put in His hands. He had the authority to judge mankind, but He didn't. Instead, he said, *"I did not come to judge the world but to save the world"* (John 12:47). Jesus showed us this overflowing love of the Father in that, though He could have judged us, He didn't. He demonstrated the Father's love to us to the "nth" degree. So I wonder why some insist on keeping the Law-giver, Judgmental view of God when Jesus clearly revealed another.

If, however, our God is not a God who is looking for ways to catch us in a fault, to snag us with one broken law, even when "caught in the very act," then perhaps salvation is more than a "ticket to heaven", an escape from Hell, or a rescue from a polluted planet. Perhaps the Father's mission is to make all things new. Not just to "turn or burn" but an endless overflow of forgiveness, healing, prosperity, deliverance, safety, rescue, liberation, preservation, soundness, restoration, and a general well-being called *Shalom*. Of course, these are all synonyms for the word we translate from the original as *salvation* (gr. "sozo"). If so, then the gifts of the Spirit play a totally different role, which we will discuss shortly.

God as Supreme Controlling Power

Here is another way we view God that affects everything else: the **Supreme controlling power.** We broadly use the term "the Sovereignty of God;" and we use it to explain the things that we can't comprehend by saying, "Well, God is in control." But too often we interpret that to mean that God has predetermined everything. In this view everything that happens is God's "choosing" and it really doesn't matter whether we participate in His plan or not. He either wills it (or "allows it") or not, and we are merely the checkers on the checkerboard being moved around by the Sovereign.

His nature is love; that is the controlling force of His sovereignty.

With this perspective, we're not sure why He wants us to pray—supposedly so we would feel like we are playing a role, but everything has been predetermined. If He wants me to be saved He'll save me. If He wants me to be Spirit-filled, He'll fill me "in His own time." If He chooses to heal me He'll heal me. If He wants to give me gifts and use me He will, but if He doesn't it must not be His will. In this view God gives the gifts to some, but not to others. And then He may decide to remove His gifts completely after a certain era. This view sees God as a unilateral actor without regard to relationship. It minimizes His desire for human partnership. In this case, why would Paul admonish the Church to *"desire (seek earnestly) the best gifts"* (1 Corinthians 14:1)?

Well, of course God is sovereign, but what does that mean? Sovereign means to act freely without constraint of a higher power or controlling force. So if God is totally free to act, how can we ever know what He will do? Some would say we can't; "you never can tell what God will do." "God works in mysterious ways, His wonders to perform." And yet He gives us promises and expects us to fully expect Him to act accordingly! So in our mechanistic, law-abiding view, we think the controlling force on God is His own words. I have heard preachers say "God has to obey His own word." No, we have to ask, where do His words come from? What determines the kind of words God speaks? It is His nature. His nature is never changing. His nature is love; that is the controlling force of His sovereignty. This means He is unconstrained and free in His way of loving freely and unceasingly. In this case, in His sovereignty He has chosen to partner with man, and He does this by freely and unceasingly giving gifts as an overflow of His compassion with power.

GOD AS DIVINE GOODIE-GIVER

Finally, some might see God as the **"divine goodie-giver"** who rewards good behavior. His blessing is reserved for the obedient ones. I have heard it said that "grace is free, but favor is earned." If this is the case, then salvation and spiritual maturity become my responsibility—to obey God. Yes, of course, I have responsibility, but it must be understood as "response –ability"—my response to what God initiates in me by the Holy Spirit (see Philippians 2:13). But in the "goodie giver" view God is after holiness and He gives us gifts as rewards for our obedience, as the proverbial carrot before the donkey. The sad result is that it reinforces a performance-based mentality and distorts the gifts of the Spirit into another exercise to prove spiritual superiority. This easily leads to the problem the Corinthians exhibited, thinking that if someone is operating in the manifestation gifts of the Spirit he is more spiritual or more holy than the rest.

But there are several problems with this view on its very face. First, the gifts of the Spirit are not the private commodity of the spiritual. Paul tells the Corinthians that he would love to treat them as spiritual people, but the problem is, they have misunderstood something very basic and done it wrong. They are not spiritual but carnal—ruled by their senses and emotions (1 Corinthians 3:1). Rather than being other-centered, loving and caring about the needs of others, they are still focused on their own way, their own rights, and their own pleasure.

I gave you milk, not solid food, for you were not yet ready for it. Indeed, you are still not ready. You are still worldly. For since there is jealousy and quarreling among you, are you not worldly? Are you not acting like mere humans? (1 Corinthians 3:2)

So clearly, the Corinthians, who "came behind in no gifts", but enjoyed an abundance of spiritually inspired utterance and knowledge, did not do so because they were the most spiritually mature or even behaved the best. It seems the Corinthians, at least some of them, were motivated by selfishness, not compassion.

Second, all such notions are based on the idea that gifts of the Spirit *belong* to certain people. But the manifestation gifts of the Spirit (1 Corinthians 12) are not the private possession of the individual believer. They are not given to the carrier or distributor of the gift, but to the person (or people) in need of the gift. They are given to the whole Church (through whoever is willing to be a conduit), as the Spirit wills, as temporary manifestations (*phanerosis*) exhibiting small facets of the Father's infinite knowledge, power and presence through the motivation of compassion.

GOD IS PERFECT, OVERFLOWING LOVE AND COMPASSION

Clearly, each of these three views contain some truth. And I acknowledge that I have cast various views in an extreme light to make a point. In reality, these views of God are embraced and lived out on a sliding scale—harsh and predetermined at one extreme, passive and capricious at the other. But my point is to demonstrate how our view of God affects our view of spiritual gifts. The question remains then, is there a more accurate view of God? What does Jesus' life, words and ministry tell us about the Father? Can we know the Father's heart? Can we know His will? If God is other than the Law-giver and Judge, the Supreme Controlling Power, or the Divine Goodie-Giver, what is He? Who is He?

Where do we get our view of God? Look carefully at these verses and let the Bible provide its own commentary:

No one has ever seen God, but God the One and Only, who is at the Father's side, has made him known (John 1:18).

Jesus answered: "Don't you know me, Philip, even after I have been among you such a long time? Anyone who has seen me has seen the Father. How can you say, 'Show us the Father'?" (John 14:9).

He [Jesus] is the image of the invisible God (Colossians 1:15).

The Son is the radiance of God's glory and the exact representation of his being (Hebrews 1:3).

In other words, Jesus is perfect theology. If you want to see what the Father is like, don't go back to the Old Testament, or even to Revelations (full of symbolism). Look at Jesus—God in the flesh. What Jesus did in both word and works is what the Father would do in the same situation if all the variables were the same.

Jesus reveals God as a three and one perfection of overflowing, other-centered love and compassion. His is not a love that is lacking any thing or needing anything. He has no ulterior motive in loving anyone. He is the All-sufficient, lacking nothing, overflowing God who cannot keep Himself to Himself, because love is by nature giving itself away (2 Corinthians 12:9; Psalm 50:7-12). He is filling up the universe with Himself, upholding all things in His relational wholeness, and filling up all free-will persons who receive Him (Ephesians 1:23; 3:10, 19; Hebrews 1:3).

Through our own brokenness we have interpreted God as a slightly better projection than our best selves. He has created man, we say, so that we would praise Him—as if He needs man's praise. But He doesn't:

He is the All-sufficient, lacking nothing, overflowing God who cannot keep Himself to Himself...

*I have no need of a bull from your stall
or of goats from your pens,
for every animal of the forest is mine,
and the cattle on a thousand hills.
I know every bird in the mountains,*

and the insects in the fields are mine.
If I were hungry I would not tell you,
for the world is mine, and all that is in it.
Do I eat the flesh of bulls
or drink the blood of goats.
"Sacrifice thank offerings to God,
fulfill your vows to the Most High,
and call on me in the day of trouble;
I will deliver you, and you will honor me." (Psalm 50:9-15
NIV)

Does God need our honor to fulfill something lacking in Him? No. He is so secure in Himself that He can give Himself completely away to you. And yet He is so non-controlling in His own completeness that He will protect your freedom to ignore Him and walk away. God is restoring all of creation back to His original intent, which is a relational wholeness that allows Him to love and fill all things freely with Himself. God is perfect, overflowing love and compassion.

So, in looking at the gifts of the Spirit, let me remind you that Jesus *"went about doing good, healing all that were sick and oppressed of the devil for God was with Him"* (Acts 10:38). Both relationality and compassion ooze from that description. Now look at these verses:

When He saw the crowds, he had compassion on them....
(Matthew 9:36)

When Jesus landed and saw a large crowd, he had compassion on them and healed their sick. (Matthew 14:14)

Jesus called his disciples to him and said, "I have compassion for these people; they have already been with me three days and have nothing to eat...." (Matthew 15:32)

Jesus had compassion on them and touched their eyes...
(Matthew 20:34)

When Jesus landed and saw a large crowd, he had
compassion on them, because they were like sheep
without a shepherd. So he began teaching them many
things. (Mark 6:34)

Do you see a common thread? Did Jesus do miracles to show
our need for forgiveness? Did He do miracles only to validate His
ministry? Did He do miracles only for the "spiritually superior"?
No. He was moved with compassion!

Picture of the Father in the Parable of the Prodigal Son

Evidently there were those in Jesus' day, just like today, that
were not connecting the dots between Jesus' actions and the
Father's loving nature. They were watching Him do miracles, heal
the sick and restore the broken, but their mental hard-drives
were so religiously formatted that they were only looking for signs
that would verify a Messiah to get them out of their immediate
political mess. So Jesus told stories—parables—many of them
about His Father, to help them put the pieces together. This is
the primary point of the story of the Prodigal. You know how the
son demands his inheritance, his comforts at the household's
expense. And after the inheritance was consumed "he comes to
his senses" and returns to his father's house. Here is where the
story would be a shocker to Jesus' hearers. Listen to it with new
ears, watch it with new eyes:

...while [the son] was still a long way off, his father saw him
and was filled with compassion for him; he ran to his son,
threw his arms around him and kissed him [and gave him
gifts]. (Luke 15:20)

What was it that caused the Father to call for the robe, the ring, the sandals and the party? It was his compassion. Compassion is the primary motivator behind all the gifts of God, including the gifts of the Spirit. Yes, there is certainly an element in the missional heart of God to partner with sons and daughters to get the work of restoration and renewal done. ...think about compassion as the "M.O.," the mode of operation of the gifts of the Spirit. Partnership is important to our relational God. Yes, there is the dimension of God's multi-faceted glory revealed in these tiny human-sized flashes of God's omnipotence, omniscience and omnipresence when He pours out rivers of power, revelation and utterance through human vessels. And that is all important. But compassion is the primary mover of Love.

WHAT IS COMPASSION?

Compassion, (Greek: *Splanchnizomai—a wrenching of the emotions or "gut"*), from a biblical perspective is more than emotion; it transcends an emotional feeling. It is a Spirit-inspired internal compulsion. It is used to describe the pain someone experiences when he has the flu, or the pain a woman experiences in labor. It is a prompting of the Holy Spirit within someone that helps him to identify with the pain of another. It is not something that can be fabricated. It is an internal drive that cannot be ignored. Now think about compassion as the "M.O.," the mode of operation of the gifts of the Spirit. It is a work of the Holy Spirit within you, by the Spirit, as the Spirit wills. Compassion stops you and says, "Do something!" The Spirit is energizing you to do something. It happens as we make ourselves available and willing before God for what He wants to do in a here-and-now situation.

How Have We Misinterpreted the Gifts?

God's nature is love, thus His primary motivation is compassion. But we have misinterpreted God's glory among us through the Orphan mindset of neediness. We feel the need for position, power, possessions and even passions. On every side we see our bankruptcy and need. We are need-minded. We've bought into a needs-driven Gospel and have sought to demonstrate its power through needs-conscious churches and church services that end with needs-driven invitations. We have pastoral leaders that need to prove they can preach moving sermons and demonstrate it by motivating many to come to the altar again. The Orphan spirit is forever coming out of the wilderness but has never quite entered into the Promised Land. Believers are told that they have authority and power in Jesus' name, but every gathering ends in an altar call with a litany of neediness and brokenness expressed. It has become normal to be needy and broken. Thus the Twentieth and Twenty-First Century Church has interpreted the gifts of the Spirit through the same self-centered lens as the First Century Church (but it's popular to speak about how immature the Corinthians were—which is, in itself, fairly carnal of us).

The saddest part is that God's people get hungry for God to show up in our generation—we rightly get tired of hearing about it only, but never seeing God move. So we are stirred to pray, to seek God, even to fast (that's when you know it's serious!). Then God shows up—He begins to manifest the gifts we long for. But we misinterpret those gifts as something we earned by our seeking God. Our Orphan heart attributes the gifts to ourselves in pride, ownership, and supposed spirituality. Then the stench that it creates drives the next generation to either discount the gifts altogether or to keep them at a comfortable distance. The cycle starts over again.

Of course, the real answer to this cycle of hot and cold is not a new revival but a revelation of the Father's heart in a spirit of Sonship. Sons are comfortable in their place in God and don't see that place as a thing to be grasped (Philippians 2:6). Sons don't have to grasp for something that is already theirs. Sons know where they came from, the authority that is theirs and where they are going—so they can serve others (John 13:1-3). A son can then be other-centered, moved with compassion for others, because he is not concerned with himself.

Then the Gifts Are Different

The Gifts of the Spirit are not just a special doctrine that some believe and others don't. They are not just the equipment of the super-spiritual to show "special forces" status. The gifts are not a sign that one church has "got it" and the others don't or one believer has it and others don't. The gifts of the Spirit are but a small part of God's continual overflow of Himself to invade broken creation with His being and bring restoration. The manifestations of the Spirit are the ongoing renewing, healing acts of Jesus by His Spirit, through His Church, to heal all that is broken, to bind up the bruised and set at liberty the captive. It is a pouring out of Himself.

If this is the case then we don't need to be overly concerned with making a mistake in "being used in the gifts" or "exercising the gifts." The gifts of the Spirit are not a test to see if you can perform. God is looking for any vessel that is willing to be a conduit of His compassion. This is why He uses some very imperfect vessels at times. This is why He uses some people that are "not cool" at times, and even "weird" to many. As one preacher said about delivery pizza, "It's not the box that makes the pizza valuable; it's the pizza that makes the box valuable. God is just looking for an empty, clean box." And even if you make a mistake in the delivery, people still see the compassion of God reaching out to them. You really cannot go wrong as long as you minister with God's heart of compassion to heal, restore and bless—Paul's prescription is "edification, exhortation and comfort."

The gifts of the Spirit are not a test to see if you can perform.

43

Prayer

Father, forgive me if I have seen you as only a Law-giver God, the Supreme Controlling Power or just a Goodie-Giver with ulterior motives. I worship You as the All Sufficient, I AM of overflowing love and compassion. Would You give me that compassionate heart to see the needs of others more than I see my own? Would you move me with compassion so that I become a conduit of your love so that even if I don't say or do everything perfectly, they experience your Love and Compassion? I earnestly desire the best gifts that will help hurting people where they are, to know You as the Healing God, as You are. In Jesus' Wonderful Name.

DISCUSSION QUESTIONS

1. According to the author what is the danger of focusing in the gifts of the Spirit?

2. Which view of God was closest to your primary concept of God? Was there a different view not mentioned?

3. Is there a difference between seeing God's gifts as a by-product of compassion versus power? What is it?

4. What did you learn from this chapter that may have sharpened your view of the Gifts of the Spirit?

Chapter Two

The Gifts of the Godhead

The Spirit is the first power we practically experience, but the last power we come to understand.
—Oswald Chambers

Our broken humanity still wants to grasp for the fruit of the knowledge of the wrong tree; we want knowledge so we can control things. But we'll never completely understand all the ways the Spirit works, nor will we control Him. But we should study carefully how He has worked through the life of Jesus and others. He is predictable only in that there is no changing of His good nature and being; and as far as information goes, that predictability is significant.

When speaking of "spiritual gifts," we must be careful to distinguish which gifts of the godhead are in view. Many combine all the gifts listed in the New Testament without distinction of which member of the Trinity they might originate or why, then adding some "gifts" (e.g. celibacy, martyrdom, artistry, etc.) that do indeed require grace (i.e. God's strength at the point of a need), but not an overflow of the nature of God in a supernatural dimension to be given to another. Spiritual gifts flow through us to bless others, especially, but not exclusively, in the context of the local church. This is why understanding the nature of God is so important. Otherwise we make three mistakes: 1) we miss the significance of God's relational nature as grounds for

Paul understands the gifts of the Spirit to be an overflow of the Triune God's infinite other-centered life... His desire to work in partnership with man, 2) we lose sight of other-centered overflowing love as the force behind the gifts and 3) we replace the supernatural with the natural. It is important to clearly articulate the nature of God as source of the gifts, and that these should not be confused with skills, talents, or natural abilities (though I am not denying that these are also gifts from God).

Do we minimize natural gifts in order to emphasize spiritual gifts? No. Michael Jordan and LeBron James, for example, demonstrate a God-given talent to play basketball. With training, that talent became a skill that has entertained millions of sports fans. Mozart had a God-given musical talent that developed into an artistry that fills the greatest concert halls in the world hundreds of years after his death. These are, undoubtedly, gifts from God; but they are not to be confused with spiritual gifts. If we want a biblical foundation, we must take Paul's distinction as a starting point.

THREE KINDS OF GIFTS

The gifts of the Spirit cannot be understood outside the context of the Triune God—the Father, Son and Holy Spirit—as the infinite, overflowing, other-centered God of love. Notice how Paul articulates the manifestations of the Spirit in the context of the Trinity in the beginning of 1 Corinthians 12:4-6:

*Now there are varieties of gifts, but the same **Spirit**; and there are varieties of service, but the same **Lord**; and there are varieties of activities, but it is the same **God** who empowers them all in everyone.*

Paul understands the gifts of the Spirit to be an overflow of the Triune God's infinite other-centered life; it flows from the same

Spirit, the same Lord, and the same God. To grasp the concept of God as the source of everything, and that all that has been made is an outflowing by-product of His being, is to understand that all of life is a gifting from God. But the Bible asserts that each of the three Persons of the godhead give specific gifts. The Father as Creator gives gifts that reveal His manifold nature; the Son gives gifts to build His Church, and the Holy Spirit gives gifts to rebuild and restore what is broken—all in compassion.

The Gifts of the Father (Motivational Gifts)

The Father, as Creator, gives gifts to mankind in the pre-wiring of each person. These gifts are found in Romans 12:6-8 and have been called the motivational gifts, as they serve as a motivational compass to the one who possesses it.

Having gifts that differ according to the grace given to us, let us use them: if prophecy, in proportion to our faith; if service, in our serving; the one who teaches, in his teaching; the one who exhorts, in his exhortation; the one who contributes, in generosity; the one who leads, with zeal; the one who does acts of mercy, with cheerfulness.

These motivational gifts are life-long gifts. They are the Spirit's "pre-wiring" or personality DNA of every person, as a bearer of the image of God. The gift is the M.O. (*modus operandi*), the way the believer will perceive and approach his/her responsibilities of life and ministry.

The Gifts of the Son (Ministry Gifts)

The Son, as Head of the Church, gives leadership gifts to the Church to build the Church into the ongoing ministry of Christ. These are found in Ephesians 4:11-12.

And he [Jesus] gave the apostles, the prophets, the evangelists, the shepherds and teachers, to equip the saints for the work of ministry, for building up the body of Christ.

The ministry (office) gifts are persons given to the Church bearing life-time "callings" to the work and using supernatural equipment to fulfill the work. The station and seasons of the calling may change or develop as a gift-mix, (i.e., a pastor may eventually move into prophetic or apostolic ministry, etc.); but the purpose doesn't change—they are given by Jesus to the Church to equip her to do the work of the ministry. A significant amount of attention could and should be focused on the restoration of these ministry gifts in the Church. I am convinced that many have abandoned the Church in frustration but can't identify the source of the frustration. They only sense that they don't fit. They don't hear a voice that resonates with the passion in their heart. I have come to believe some of this frustration is because we have forced the five ministry gifts to operate in the wineskin of only two—the pastor and teacher. This will have to be treated in another work.

The Gifts of the Spirit (Manifestation Gifts)

The Holy Spirit, as the life of the Church, comes to bring the Church to her ultimate spiritual wholeness, maturity and purpose. These manifestation gifts are found in 1 Corinthians 12:7-11, and are the primary focus of this study.

To each is given the manifestation of the Spirit for the common good. For to one is given through the Spirit the utterance of wisdom, and to another the utterance of knowledge according to the same Spirit, to another faith by the same Spirit, to another gifts of healing by the one Spirit, to another the working of miracles, to another prophecy, to another the ability to distinguish between spirits, to another various kinds of tongues, to another the interpretation of tongues. All these are empowered by one and the same Spirit, who apportions to each one individually as he wills.

The manifestation gifts are not the possession of the believer, rather an occasional enablement to dispense the Spirit's compassion via power to a particular need. The manifestation (*phanerosis*) gifts are not distributed as the believer wills but as the Spirit wills. They are given to meet a particular need, and Holy Spirit is the one who chooses which gift to give for the particular occasion.

The Western mindset has interpreted these gifts either as mechanical operations of God or antiquated operations that have ceased altogether. In reality, these gifts are an ongoing, infinite overflow of God's other-centered nature, which means that all three members of the Trinity are constantly pouring forth gifts in order to bring the Church and the world to fulfillment of the Father's purpose.

Dr. C. Peter Wagner says, *"a spiritual gift is a special attribute (strength or ability) given by the Holy Spirit to every member of the Body of Christ according to God's grace for use within the context of the Body."*

Dr. Lester Sumrall defines spiritual gifts as *"spiritual, not soulish in nature; an extraordinary ability that is bestowed upon a human being by the infinite strength and power of the Holy Ghost."*

Dr. Jack Hayford defines spiritual gifts as, *"a free gift, a spiritual endowment, a miraculous faculty."*

It is important to note that the gifts of the Spirit are just that—spiritual. They are not heightened human abilities. Spiritual gifts are not God helping man to be the best he can be at a human level; they are supernatural endowments enabling man to be better than he can be. There is a supernatural element to these that can never be achieved by human effort. This can be seen clearly in the words Paul uses to describe the gifts.

The two primary words used for spiritual gifts in the original language are *"charisma"* and *"pneumatikos."* The root word of charisma is *"charis"* which simply means "grace." Grace is most often defined as "God's unmerited favor"—and it certainly is. Grace is God's free gift to mankind, birthed out of His overflowing, other-centered nature. But we often miss the significance of grace unless we see how Jesus defines it.

Jesus' provides a definition of grace when responding to Paul's appeal for relief from the demonic opposition that stirred up trouble everywhere he went. He petitioned the Lord three times for deliverance. Notice what Jesus says, *"My grace is sufficient for you, for My strength is made perfect in your weakness* [at the point of your need]" (2 Corinthians 12:9). Jesus defines grace as "God's strength (supernatural supply) at the point of our need." It is God doing for us what we could not do for ourselves. We are saved by grace—God himself did for us what we could never do for ourselves, and He gave it freely. We can't earn it, and we can't work for it. That is grace.

Now let's apply His definition to spiritual graces (*pneumatikos charis*). It makes perfect sense to understand spiritual gifts as "a special attribute" or "an extraordinary ability" at the point of a need. The root word for pneumatikos is "pneuma" which means spirit. This may refer to the human spirit or the Holy Spirit, but in most occasions when referring to the Holy Spirit the Greek will specify *Hagios* (holy) *Pneuma* (spirit). Either way, *pneumatikos* points us to the fact that these gifts (strengths, abilities) are not physical, natural, soulish, or emotional in nature and origin; they are spiritual and function through the human spirit by the Holy Spirit. It is God doing for us (and through us) what we could never do ourselves. And they are provided as an overflow of God's compassionate nature to meet a human need.

> *Those who attempt to teach about spiritual gifts but have little experience in the things of the Spirit will invariably apply the operation of some of the gifts to natural abilities...*

This may not seem to be an important distinction, but it is. Those who attempt to teach about spiritual gifts but have little experience in the things of the Spirit will invariably apply the operation of some of the gifts to natural abilities (i.e. prophecy is nothing more than preaching, the gift of the word of knowledge is equivalent to going to college, etc.). However, preaching can be learned and exercised intellectually without the aid of the Holy Spirit or the function of the human spirit. We have all heard that kind of preaching at some time or another. Therefore, some preaching can be prophetic, but prophecy is not preaching. Be wary of sitting under teaching about spiritual gifts by naturally gifted teachers that have never been exposed to the operation of those gifts in the church. To use a baseball analogy, I can tell you the difference between a fastball and a curve ball as I sit on my couch and watch the game on TV, but that doesn't mean I've ever stood in the batter's box and felt a 95 mph bullet fly past my head. Experience and observation from a distance are two very different things. With that being said, just because a person has stood in a batter's box and experienced a fastball, doesn't mean he knows how to hit the ball. It requires a combination of exposure, experience, and understanding.

Therefore, my working definition is as follows:

"A spiritual gift is a supernatural enablement by the Holy Spirit via the recreated human spirit to bring God's strength and presence to the point of human need."

DISCUSSION QUESTIONS

1. Why is it so important to understand the nature of God as demonstrated by the gifts of the godhead?

2. What are the three consequences the author enumerates if we fail to understand God's nature of love as the driver of the gifts?

3. Why is Jesus' definition of grace significant to the issue of the gifts of the Spirit?

PART II - MANIFESTATION GIFTS

CHAPTER THREE

GETTING TO KNOW THE MANIFESTATION GIFTS

As a reminder, when we talk about Gifts of the Spirit, we are referring to the Manifestation Gifts mentioned in 1 Corinthians 12:7-11:

To each is given the manifestation of the Spirit for the common good. For to one is given through the Spirit the utterance of wisdom, and to another the utterance of knowledge according to the same Spirit, to another faith by the same Spirit, to another gifts of healing by the one Spirit, to another the working of miracles, to another prophecy, to another the ability to distinguish between spirits, to another various kinds of tongues, to another the interpretation of tongues. All these are empowered by one and the same Spirit, who apportions to each one individually as he wills.

Paul lists nine manifestations of the Spirit to bring edification, exhortation and comfort to the church, and these are easily grouped into three categories:

1. **Revelation gifts** (utterance [word] of wisdom, utterance [word] of knowledge, distinguishing of spirits),

2. **Power gifts** (special faith, healings, and working of miracles), and

3. **Utterance gifts** (prophecy, various kinds of tongues, and interpretation of tongues).

DIVERSITY OF GIFTS

To help us understand these gifts, we must first see them in their literary context: 1 Corinthians 12:4-6:

There are diversities of gifts, but the same Spirit. There are differences of ministries, but the same Lord. And there are diversities of activities, but it is the same God who works all in all.

Differences of Ministries (*diakonia*): Serving happens in different ways through different people. The gifts will look different as they function through different people's personalities, knowledge-level, congregational context, and motivational gifting. This is part of the glory of God's working through man—He chooses to work and speak through the prism of human complexity. What is important to note is that those who minister gifts to others in the Body of Christ should not be treated as celebrities for doing so, but as servants—waiters and waitresses bringing food to the table—from God's kitchen to the table of broken and hungry lives.

Diversities of Activities (*energema*): The intensity (energy), breadth, and scope of the gifts will vary as well. Other translations interpret this word as "operations" which speaks to a variety of ways things can be done. Because the gifts function through human beings with all our uniqueness and complexities, they are subject to individual limitations (personality, knowledge, boldness, faith, etc.). Paul says in 1 Corinthians 14:32 that "the spirits of the prophets are subject to the prophets."

So it may seem there is a conflict; I have said that these gifts are given by the Sprit as He wills. They are not to be used at our whim or discretion. And I am also saying that the gifts are subject to the person using them, (i.e. the spirit of the prophet is subject to the prophet). But both are true—it's not a paradox but a partnership. As Jean Darnall says:

If Holy Spirit uses you frequently in a particular gift, it can be recognized as a ministry, and you can steward it by developing it. It's more appropriate to say that someone has a ministry of... than that the person has a gift of.... The gifts are not for the person, but flow through the person for those who need it. The effectiveness of the ministry of these gifts can be improved upon with experience, frequency, and maturity.[3]

So the Holy Spirit is looking for those who will desire to be used, and be available. But most importantly, the motivation of the heart (either love or pride) has impact on what is produced and imparted.

In the next chapters we will get more acquainted with these operations of blessing that come from the Holy Spirit to strengthen the Church.

DISCUSSION QUESTIONS

1. What is the difference between diversities of ministries (*diakonia*) and activities (*energema*)?

2. Can you think of an example of the same gift looking very different when in operation through different people?

3. Why is it important to understand that there is room for different kinds of operations and "intensities"?

CHAPTER FOUR

REVELATION GIFTS

THE UTTERANCE (WORD) OF WISDOM

During my pastorate in Houston, Texas, a middle-aged couple slipped into the Wednesday night service and settled on the back row while I was teaching. I had never seen them before, but the Holy Spirit began to single the couple out to me and a direction-shaping word began to form in my heart. After the service had concluded I just knew enough to know I was supposed to minister to them. I walked to the back and introduced myself. "Can I pray with you?" I asked. They warmly responded and as I began to pray, the Lord began to speak to me about the man's future. I didn't know if they had any background in the things of the Spirit, but I knew that people don't attend a new church on a Wednesday night unless they are looking for something. In addition, I carry a sense that people are much more open to the things of the Spirit than many give them credit for. People are spirit beings, hard-wired for the supernatural. I said to the gentleman, "The Lord is giving you a vision and a design, but there are many obstacles. But if you will press through and not waver the funding will come and what God has put in your heart will be completed."

No matter how many times a person has been used of the Lord like this there is always the lingering question, "What if I am totally off-base here?" I didn't know what the word meant to the man but later found out that he had developed a huge retirement resort center that would house a small hospital filled with doctors' offices and therapy clinics. The doctors who had lined up to invest had become anxious and many had withdrawn their funds. Unfortunately, the building had already begun and had come to a stalemate. This gentleman was at the end of his emotional rope. He came to the service that night asking God to speak to him. Without any knowledge of the man or the situation, God gave me enough to give him encouragement and some direction. He went back to his investors with a new boldness and they signed on again and he completed that massive project—and began to attend our church.

What I did not know at the time was that this huge retirement resort center was being built less than three blocks from the church, and in fact, to this day one can sit in the pastor's office of that church where I used to sit, look out the window and see that Retirement Center five stories high only a couple of blocks away. Needless to say, there were many occasions after that night, when I needed my own encouragement and inspiration. I would open the blinds to my office, look out the window and see that massive Retirement Center as a testament to the gifts of the Spirit as God's compassion to help and heal.

We can define the gift of the word of wisdom as a revelation in fraction, or in part—like one word is to a paragraph or book—of the mind of God concerning people, places, or things pertaining to the future as they pertain to understanding the unfolding of the purposes of God and how one can cooperate with those purposes. Jesus told us that the Holy Spirit would teach us all things and show us things yet to come (John 16:13).

The gift of the word of wisdom has little to do with natural wisdom, highly developed intellect, or years of experience. It is an occasional supernatural endowment, a word for a given situation or era which may or may not be given for the purpose speaking it out to others. In other words, this gift may function in conjunction with prophecy if it is spoken to others, but it may be a word given to a person to assist that person in cooperating or interceding for the unfolding of God's plans and purpose. It differs from the gift of the word of knowledge in that it pertains to the development of future plans and purposes of God (rather than a knowledge of past or present events), and usually advises man's role in partnering or preparing for those purposes. It may come in picture form, as a word or phrase, or as dreams or visions, etc.

In the story I shared earlier, the gift was a word of wisdom because it helped unfold the future of God's plans and purposes not only for this man but for the many people that the Retirement Center will yet touch. Because it was given to me to speak out to him, its operation was a combination of a word of wisdom and gift of prophecy. But sometimes God will give a word of wisdom—something concerning the purposes of God for the future—that is not to be spoken out prophetically. Many times God needs someone who will pray something into being, and sometimes that requires the discipline to keep quiet about some things that are not yet "ripe" in the spirit.

I was pastoring in Azle, Texas, in the mid-to-late 1980's and the Lord was blessing the church with considerable growth. I began to look for a piece of property on the highway that would be more visible and accessible to the Fort Worth-side of that small community. One day, driving from Fort Worth into Azle on Hwy 199, my attention was captivated by a rising slope on the right-hand side of the highway. Something dropped into my "knower" (my spirit) that said, "That is your property." So I found out who owned the property and made contact. To my disappointment, they had no interest in selling.

I have found that moving in the gifts of the Spirit involve faith, tenacity, and an ability to sort out the difference between emotion and spirit. I have had very few occasions that I was not challenged emotionally (perhaps with fear and self-doubt, disappointment, and certainly frustration) by something God gave me to do or say. To walk in the Spirit means to stand confident in what you know in your "knower" even when the circumstances seem to scream to the contrary.

I was perplexed and disappointed by the adamant nature of the property owner's unwillingness to even consider selling. But

I did what I knew to do: I went out on the property and walked around it, and all over it, praying in the spirit. I contacted the owner again, and again the property owner was not interested. I said little to anyone else about it because I didn't want to stir expectations prematurely.

Time was of the essence for our young congregation and we entertained other options. During this same time, another church in the area had encountered difficulties resulting in a dwindling of families and resources to the point they needed to sell their property. Unfortunately, it was on the backside of town and on a dirt road that spelled oblivion to my entrepreneurial mind. But I found myself in the property owner's shoes now, being approached but not interested. At the urging of my team I finally met with the board of the small congregation and, to make the story brief, they gave us the church and 6 acres of property for what was owed against it (just over $40,000) and we were able to take up payments with no money down. It was an amazing financial miracle, but in the back of my mind I wondered "where I missed it" regarding the other piece of property.

Fast-forward 20 years. I had raised up another pastor-couple to lead that church and I was speaking at the church's 20th Anniversary. The pastor says, "Kerry, I've been telling you about a piece of property that we've been looking to purchase. We just signed a contract on it and I want to show it to you." I was excited for them. They had been on the backside for a long time. He drove me out to the highway, and we happily discussed the good things the Lord was doing in the church. As he pulled the car off the side of the road and to a stop, he must have seen my mouth drop open because he said, "What's wrong?"

I said, "You've got to be kidding me! Paul, do you realize this is the same piece of property I saw twenty years ago, and the Lord said "This is your property"? I walked this property in prayer but could never get the owner to sell!"

There is an even more remarkable part of that story that has to do with mineral rights and why the Lord didn't want me to mess up His plans by building on it in the late '80s. The Abbey, in Azle, Texas, led by pastors Paul and PerriAnne Brownback, is now thriving with His blessing. And evidently, the are some things about our partnership with God and the gifts that have an element of mystery. Even if we don't understand everything He is doing he wants us to partner with Him. I just needed to play my small part, which was to pray, stake a claim in the spirit, and (in this instance) not say too much before the appropriate time. The gift of a word of wisdom, like all the gifts, can take on many forms and functions, as the Scripture calls it "diversities of operations."

Biblical Example:

Think about the powerful example Paul receiving a word of wisdom during a sea storm—a gift to all those that sailed with him—that all would be spared and that he would stand before Caesar (Acts 27:23-25). Not only did the word give hope to the sailors (and prisoners) that they would live, but it confirmed the plans and purposes for Paul that he would bear witness of Jesus Christ in the more important city of the world at that time. In the process, that word for all practical purposes elevated Paul as the captain of the ship—giving directions as to what should be done and what would happen as a result. The word of wisdom has to do with the plans and purposes of God for the future.

Other Examples:

- God reveals His plans and purposes to Noah regarding the flood (Genesis 6:12-13).

- David prophesies through the Psalms how Messiah would come and die (Psalm 2; Psalm 22).

- Solomon gives instruction to divide the baby, knowing the real mother would react with compassion (1 Kings 3:16-28).

- Jesus tells of the destruction of the Temple and signs of His return (Matthew 24; Luke 21).

- Jesus tells the disciples to find a colt for His entry to Jerusalem, where and who (Mark 11:1-2).

- Ananias receives instruction to minister to Saul of Tarsus and what the results will be (Acts 9:11-16).

THE UTTERANCE (WORD) OF KNOWLEDGE

I was having lunch in a little cafe in Azle, Texas, minding my own business. I began to notice a man sitting at a table across the cafe with his work buddies. These men were wearing work uniforms with their names on a label on the front of the shirt. The more my attention was drawn to this short, stout man, the more I realized the Holy Spirit was trying to tell me something. As I listened I heard the Lord say, "He is running from a call." I knew what He meant, though I was not given specific words. I knew in my spirit that the man had been called into the ministry as a young boy, but was running from that call.

I asked the Lord, "So what do you want me to do about that?" The thought persisted but it was just a thought "He's running from a call." As I was finishing my lunch I said, "Lord, if you want me to speak to him You're going to have to set up the situation. I don't want to embarrass him in front of his work buddies. If you arrange it so that I get to talk with him privately, I'll talk with him."

I finished my meal and went to the counter to pay for my meal, as usual. While I was waiting for the cashier to add up the tab I turned around and this man was standing right behind me. I felt uncertain and hesitant, but I turned to the man and said, "I need to talk to you for a second. Can we meet outside?" He looked at me quizzically but nodded affirmatively.

I waited for him outside, introduced myself and called him by name; (That wasn't a word of knowledge; His name was on his shirt). I simply said, "While I was eating I felt like the Lord spoke to me about you." I had deduced that if he had already heard a "call" on his life, he knew enough about God that this wouldn't be strange language to him. "You know the Lord but you've been running from a call on your life for the ministry." As soon as I said it he bowed his head and tears welled up in his eyes. He said, "I know it. But how did you know that?" I said, "Evidently the Lord cares about you very much and He's calling you to finish what He started in you. You know the gifts and callings of God are irrevocable." That was it. No lightning bolts—no altar call on the sidewalk. He expressed thanks and we parted.

You see, it's not our job to make something happen in that instance. We are just the messengers, bringing God's love to someone who has probably bought into a lie of the enemy that God is mad at him or doesn't love him anymore. There are a lot of people out there just like that man, who need to know that God still loves them. I don't know the end of that story but I do know that the Lord loves that man so much that he sent a stranger to remind him of something He had said in his youth. It is the Lord's compassion that is the driver behind the gifts of the Spirit.

We can define the gift of the word or utterance of knowledge as a word that reveals a fact or fraction of God's knowledge concerning people and situations in the past or present. It may involve the diagnosis of a problem, a sickness identified, or any fact that would be otherwise unknown to the person receiving the word as a gift for another. It is not to be confused with education or intellect; nor is it attained through natural means of study, reading, observation or experience. It is knowledge (about something that exists or did exist, something that is happening or did happen) that is given by the Holy Spirit in the spirit of man. It is an occasional supernatural endowment, a word for a given situation or era. It may or may not be given for the purpose of utterance or declaring to others and it may come in the form of a picture, words, vision, a dream or just an impression. It may be an awareness of a situation or a person that needs someone to intercede for them, or to change a decision or pending plan.

When my dad, Max, was twenty-one and attending his first semester at an engineering trade school in Chicago the Lord spoke to him and said, "You need to go home now." It didn't make any sense and it certainly wasn't convenient in those days. It meant missing days of class and the unexpected expense and discomfort of a bus trip from Chicago back to the Texas panhandle. But he obeyed, bought the ticket, called the local home grocer who had the only phone in town, and left word that he was coming home.

When he arrived home his parents asked. "Your school term isn't over yet—why did you come home?" they asked. "I don't know," Max said, "I just know I was supposed to come home." The next day was Sunday and the family went to church together. On Monday morning they ate breakfast together and his dad left for work. Thirty minutes later a man came to the door and said, "Your dad is really sick. You better come." Dad's father had suffered a massive heart attack. He died on the way to the hospital.

We could speculate that the Lord wouldn't tell my dad to go home unless he was supposed to raise his dad from death or intercede to avoid the situation. Those are possibilities; but what is significant to this story was that my dad's mom was not left alone. Think of God's compassion. In the hour of her crisis and grief the Lord's compassion moved the son to be home. And he stayed there and cared for her. It makes me wonder how many times the Lord's compassion went out to protect someone, cover someone, be with someone, but we dismissed that still small voice as an abstract thought. How often then has our miss been interpreted as a lie about God's absence? I believe God is always speaking and always giving gifts even if we don't recognize them.

Biblical Example:

Remember when Elijah had conquered the prophets of Baal but then ran for his life from the threats of Jezebel? He needed encouragement in the midst of his depression under the juniper tree. God gave him a word of knowledge *"I have yet 7,000 who will not bow their knee to Baal..."* (1 Kings 19:18). That word of knowledge brought Elijah to a clearer perspective.

Other Examples:

- Elisha receives supernatural information about Gehazi taking the inappropriate gifts (2 Kings 5:20-27).

- Jesus tells the Samaritan woman, *"You have had five husbands and the one you are now with is not your husband..."* (John 4:18-19).

- Peter receives by a word of knowledge by vision, *"Behold, three men seek thee. Rise and go down and accompany them without hesitation, for I have sent them"* (Acts 10:19-20).

DISTINGUISHING OF SPIRITS

Only once have I seen the appearance of a demonic spirit and it was such a brief encounter while praying in solitude in the church auditorium I was pastoring in at the time, it might not qualify as the operation of a gift. Neither was it a face-to-face encounter, though I have had numerous occasions to minister deliverance to those oppressed by demons.

Have you ever seen an angel? There was an old cowboy who went by the name "Cotton." He wasn't serving God but his wife was ceaseless in her prayers and enlisting the church to pray for him. One Saturday night while he was just dozing off to sleep he was startled by someone who had come into his room and grabbed him by the ankle. It was an angelic being that called him by name and said, "It's time. Tomorrow you go to church."

It shook up this old rodeo-rider cowboy so much that he had to get up, make a cup of coffee and sit on the porch and ponder

This gift is about seeing in the spirit dimension. It is an occasional ability to see into the spirit world— angels, demons, or the Lord himself. what had just happened. He finally settled down enough to go back to bed. When he woke up the next morning he rationalized that he had possibly been dreaming, and decided to stick with his Sunday morning routine and do some work on his barn. He leaned a ladder against the roof of the barn and was climbing the ladder when his wife got in the car and headed to church. Suddenly a large hand grabbed his ankle again and he almost took a dive off the ladder. The same angel was below him on the ladder saying, "Now. It's time," in a very serious voice. Then the angel disappeared.

The old cowboy, shaken again, jumped off the ladder, ran into the house, changed clothes and arrived at the church in the middle of the worship songs. He didn't wait for the pastor to preach a sermon. He headed straight down the aisle and knelt at the front. "I have to give my heart to Jesus, and I have to do it now!" That was the beginning of his new life in Jesus.

This gift is about seeing in the spirit dimension. It is an occasional ability to see into the spirit world—angels, demons, or the Lord himself. It is an ability to distinguish, perceive or differentiate the identity of the spirits that are causing different manifestations or conditions.

It is not clairvoyance or witchcraft (which is by the operation of demons), ESP or mental telepathy. It is not the gift of "discernment" or the gift of suspicion or speculation; and neither is it to be confused with fault-find, judging, or discerning of character. It may or may not be given for the purpose of utterance or declaring to others. The perception into the spirit world will usually reveal the cause behind a person or group's behavior or thinking in the natural world.

Biblical Examples:

A very clear demonstration of this gift is seen when Paul is being followed by the girl with a spirit of divination (Acts 16:16-18).

As we were going to the place of prayer, we were met by a slave girl who had a spirit of divination and brought her owners much gain by fortune-telling. She followed Paul and us, crying out, "These men are servants of the Most High God, who proclaim to you the way of salvation." And this she kept doing for many days. Paul, having become greatly annoyed, turned and said to the spirit, "I command you in the name of Jesus Christ to come out of her." And it came out that very hour.

Why do you suppose Paul allowed the girl to provide the bad advertising for "many days"? He certainly wouldn't want a demon-possessed person associated with his ministry. Jesus always told the demons to be quiet. Do you suppose it was a matter of his patience wearing thin; he put up with it as long as he could? Or was it a matter of waiting for the Holy Spirit to show him exactly what he was dealing with? Notice he didn't speak to the girl—he spoke to the spirit that was driving the girl. Paul knew that the gifts of the Spirit do not work as the person wills but as the Spirit wills. He was careful to avoid the iniquity of self-initiated, unauthorized ministry (Matthew 7:23) and we should be too. We cannot make the gifts function at our whim, though we can learn to minister more and more effectively in partnership with our compassionate God.

Other Examples:

• Jesus identifies a spirit of infirmity and looses a daughter of Abraham (Luke 13:16).

- Jesus casts out spirits with a word (Matt. 8:16-17) and clearly carries on a conversation with Satan in the desert temptations (Luke 4:1-12).

- Simon the sorcerer wants the power to disburse Spirit-fullness to people but Peter sees he is full of a different spirit (Acts 8:20-23).

DISCUSSION QUESTIONS

1. What is the difference between the gift of the word of wisdom and the gift of the word of knowledge?

2. Have you ever experienced either giving or receiving one of the revelation gifts?

3. How is the discerning (seeing) of spirits a gift of God's compassion? Can you give a biblical example?

CHAPTER FIVE

POWER GIFTS

SPECIAL FAITH

The manifestation gift of special faith is a release of an unlimited faith on certain occasions by the Holy Spirit, which supernaturally accomplishes what is impossible through mere human faith. Though I have not had as much experience with this gift personally, it seems the operation of this gift suspends all doubt and unbelief in the heart of the one who is partnering with God for the benefit of others.

This gift is not to be confused with saving faith which every believer has, or the general measure of faith which every person possesses (Ephesians 2:8; Romans 12:3; Acts 16:30-31). It is not to be confused with the faith that is obtained by hearing God's Word (Romans 10:17). Every Christian has faith, but the gift of special faith is in operation as the Spirit wills (1 Corinthians 12:9, 11). Special faith has nothing to do with an individual's ability or capacity to believe (strong faith vs. weak faith), but is a supernatural endowment for a special occasion and often works in conjunction with working of miracles (e.g. raising the dead).

A classic story of the gift of faith is demonstrated through the life of Smith Wigglesworth. He tells the story in his sermon entitle "The Power of Christ's Resurrection:"

One morning about eleven o'clock I saw a woman who was suffering with a tumor. She could not live through the day. A little blind girl led me to the bedside. Compassion broke me up and I wanted that woman to live for the child's sake. I said to the woman, "Do you want to live?" She could not speak. She just moved her finger. I anointed her with oil and said, "In the name of Jesus." There was a stillness of death that followed; and the pastor, looking at the woman, said to me, "She is gone."

When God pours in compassion it has resurrection power in it. I carried that woman across the room, put her against the wardrobe and held her there. I said, "In the name of Jesus, death, come out." And soon her body began to tremble like a leaf. "In Jesus' name, walk," I said. She did and went back to bed.[4]

It is a gift of faith in operation when you know what to do and have no doubt that it is God doing the work. You don't prop a dead woman up against the wardrobe and command her to come to life if you're just trying to make it work. It's not a sin to struggle with doubt in our mind, but if you are struggling with doubts, it's probably not the gift of faith. But notice carefully what moved the gift of faith into operation. It was the overflowing compassion of God that came into an uneducated plumber's soul and made him a carrier of the precious gift of life to this mother and her daughter.

Biblical Example:

Stephen saw heaven opened and forgives in the midst of martyrdom (Acts 7:54-60). That was a special exercise of faith working in conjunction with the distinguishing of spirits—in this case, it was the resurrected Christ, giving Stephen a standing ovation at the right hand of the Father.

Other Examples:

- Elijah is sustained in the wilderness, fed by ravens (1 Kings 17).

- Daniel is clearly sustained with a supernatural faith in the lion's den (Daniel 6:16-22).

- The three Hebrew children walk into a fiery furnace with a sense of calm, divine composure (Daniel 3:19-20).

- Peter has the faith to step out of the boat and walk on water (Matthew 14:22-33).

- Elisha throws a stick into the water and causes the ax head to float (2 Kings 6:5-6).

- Jesus walks on the water (Mark 4:45-48).

- Jesus raises Lazarus from the dead with no sense of pressure or anxiety to perform (John 11:43-44).

You have noticed that the examples being given are both from the Old and New Testaments. We would do well to understand the difference between Old Testament examples of the miraculous, where the Old Testament prophets had the Spirit come upon them occasionally, and the New Testament experiences where the Holy Spirit lives within the believer permanently. This distinction could lead some to assume that New Testament believers can "move in the gifts" whenever they want. And yet even in this new dispensation (to use the word loosely) the manifestations of the Spirit function similarly to Old Testament (i.e. a supernatural endowment for a temporary occasion). These manifestation gifts are not the permanent possession of the believer, but temporary empowering for a particular situation. This is not to say the Holy Spirit doesn't want to distribute gifts all the time to everyone—it is to say that

He alone knows when a person is ready to receive it and how to administer those gifts in ways that maximize kingdom impact.

If the manifestation gifts are the personal possession of believers, to be used at will, then those believers would be criminal if they refuse to empty out every hospital immediately by healing every sick person. But these work as the Spirit wills.

WORKING OF MIRACLES

One of the great modern day miracles happened in the basement of a church. A man had died from a car accident and lay in a casket for three days. His wife refused to bury him, but insisted on taking him to the church where Reinhard Bonnke was preaching. The attendants wouldn't let her bring the coffin into the auditorium but took the body out of the coffin and into the basement. While Bonnke was preaching (not knowing of the dead man under the auditorium), the man began to breathe again and after some time jumped off the table upon which he had been placed. This miracle and others are well documented and can be Googled (see Raised from the dead—Bonnke). Why is it easier for us to believe it could happen 2,000 years ago, but not today?

The gift of the working of miracles has to do with a superseding of natural laws. We have come to call them "laws of nature" though they are, of course, laws of God for the physical universe. The working of miracles is a momentary delegation of authority over the natural course of events or temporary suspension of the natural law that allows an exercise of Divine energy beyond human capacities. This might include creative miracles in the human body. Miracles are releases of God's power or energy (*energema*) which produce an extraordinary result or phenomena as far as man is concerned; but ordinary with God. This gift is often in tandem operation with the gift of faith or gift of healings. For example, if someone is born blind or lame, the physical parts may all be present, but if they have never been used (e.g. the muscles in the eye or the legs) then the working of miracles and a gift of healing are in operation together to enable muscle to suddenly be able to function. These are the "power gifts"—they do something *It is important to be around people of faith.* supernatural. This gift usually requires partnership with a person who has come past certain barriers of people-fear or political correctness (Hebrews 6:4-8).

The primary purpose is, of course, the release of God's compassion, but in connection with the preaching of the Gospel to confirm God's message to unbelieving people (Acts 2:22). It is a needed tool in the ministry of the evangelist and apostle (1 Corinthians 12:27-28) and as such can become an accompanying sign gift that the minister can develop and increase with use. But it is not restricted to "ministers" per se. Though some miracles require no human intermediary (e.g. Balaam's donkey, Numbers 22), the working of miracles is the manifestation of God's power by the Spirit through human agency.

It is important to be around people of faith. It is important to build a track record of faith and the miraculous if you want to partner with God to express His compassionate heart.

During my elementary school years I attended Hiway Temple Assemblies of God, in Odessa, Texas, pastored by Cecil and Daisy Gillock. Daisy was the sister of missionary evangelist T.L. Osborn. I grew up hearing stories about the miracles that T.L. Osborn would experience in his massive outreaches around the world. But the greatest impact on my life as a youngster was the living and ongoing testimony of Ronnie Coyne.

When Ronnie was just a boy he suffered an infection in his right eye due to a childhood accident. A neighbor was swinging a wire around over his head and poked Ronnie in the eye. The eye became so infected that it had to be removed and a plastic prosthetic eyeball was inserted.

My pastor, Daisy Gillock, was preaching a revival in Oklahoma shortly after that event and little Ronnie came up for prayer—not for the blind eye but for problems with his tonsils. She prayed for the tonsils but then noticed that the eye "didn't look right." Ronnie told her that he was blind in that eye. But before anyone could tell her it wasn't a real eye, she placed her hands on each side of his head, with her thumbs over the eyes, and commanded the eye to receive sight. The audience gasped, knowing the boy's condition. What happened next was one of the greatest perpetual miracles in modern times. There were numerous front page newspaper stories in the Oklahoma papers in 1950 and 1951 heralding the event and you can Google "Ronnie Coyne" today and find his story. One of those sites reads:

Ronald Coyne was prayed for by a lady evangelist who didn't know he had a plastic eye. The evangelist prayed for him to receive his sight in Jesus' Name, and a miracle happened. From that time, he could see through an empty socket, with his "good" eye taped over in every way possible.

Because my pastor was that "lady evangelist," Ronnie, now a grown man when I was a kid, came to our church every year to preach and to demonstrate the ongoing miracle. My dad was one of the men who would take handkerchiefs, tape them over his good eye until he looked like a wounded soldier returning from war. Ronnie would then tell folks to bring anything with the smallest print possible to the front. He would hold the empty eye-socket open and read tiny words off of little pencils, business cards and postcards... with miraculous sight out of an empty eye-socket. He would hold up his right hand, palm facing forward and slightly cupped and say, "It is no different than seeing out of the palm of your hand. God can do it any way He wants to." Then he would preach about the miraculous power of God and people would get saved and healed in every service.

You can imagine the impact that had on this grade-school kid, seeing this miracle year after year. Why would it seem strange for me to believe God would do the same through me or anyone else who would partner with Him to minister compassion with power to people?

During my Bible college days, when I was studying seriously the things of faith, I was working my way through school by parking cars as a valet attendant at restaurants. One night a college friend and I were working at a fancy restaurant. The challenge with parking cars at a restaurant is that the crowd tends to arrive all at once and leave all at once. On one particular night the crowd had arrived and we had the cars parked. The work pace was in a lull before the storm, literally. We knew the crowds would be exiting the restaurant in about an hour. Our income was based on tips, so bringing the cars up quickly is essential to have a good night financially.

Then we looked across the freeway and saw a massive wall of rain coming toward the restaurant. We knew this would ruin our night. If all of the people came out of the restaurant to collect their car in pouring rain, they would get impatient and run get their own cars (I know, it doesn't make sense). If they got impatient, we would lose our income. I told my friend, "Let's speak to this storm and command it to go around us." We were just learning to exercise faith, but I was raised seeing bold faith. We walked out to the edge of the parking lot, pointed at the wall of rain coming our direction and said, "In the name of Jesus, we command you to go around this restaurant. Not one drop of rain will come on this property until we have finished our job." And we spoke with the boldest voice of authority we could muster. Jerry Vaughn (now a powerful missionary to the nations) and I stepped back toward the restaurant and watched the wall of rain continue to come across the freeway toward the property.

Suddenly as the rain got to the edge of the property it was as though a curtain was pulled open; the clouds parted. We watched the wall of water split in two directions and go on either side around our property. An hour later the property was still dry and everything around the property was drenched with a Texas downpour. We were able to get the cars to patrons in a timely way and made the income that we needed that night. But more importantly, we saw God's miraculous power working through two Bible college boys and it helped build a track record faith for the future.

Yes we were young, and yes, it may have seemed crazy or foolish to some. But I saw a miracle with my own eyes and that experience became a huge boost of confidence in my walk of faith in God. That event has come to mind on numerous occasions— bones being reset in a leg, and eyesight without an eyeball— when I have come to opportunities to exercise faith and partner with the Spirit of God. And God doesn't change—He wants to do the same for a new generation.

Biblical Examples:

Biblical examples of miracles are commonplace, even though Old Testament miracles happened mostly through a special class of prophets because the Holy Spirit had not yet been *"poured out on all flesh"* (Joel 2:28).

- Moses and Aaron perform many miracles before Pharaoh, and with his rod he parts the Red Sea (Exodus 7-11).

- Elijah with his cloak, divides waters so Elijah and Elisha can cross (2 Kings 2:8).

- Samson kills 1,000 men with the jawbone of a donkey (Judges 15:14-15).

- Jesus turns water into wine (John 2:1-11).

- Jesus multiplies bread and fish to feed thousands (Matthew 14:13-21).

- Paul's "special miracles" (*dunamis-power*) seem to work in conjunction with gift of healings (Acts 19:11-12). These clearly help confirm his apostleship and aid his ministry to evangelize and establish churches in new territories.

GIFTS OF HEALING

Gifts of healing can be defined as a supernatural impartation on occasions to heal a myriad of types of diseases, sometimes limited to specific kinds, sometimes in-mass, but in greater measure or intensity than regular faith can accomplish and usually requiring no faith on the part of the sick. These gifts of healing could be considered similar in operation to what happened on occasion at the Pool of Bethesda (John 5:2-4).

It is not to be confused with healing via faith in God's Word. It is not to be confused with the practice of medicine, though God in His limitless compassion, also uses doctors. It is not the regular healing ministry of Jesus administered by believers through faith in the name of Jesus (Mark 16:17-18). This gift may operate through the voice of command (Matthew 8:16-17), via tangible materials like handkerchiefs and aprons (Acts 19:12), or through the laying on of hands (Acts 9:17-18). Note that there were times when Jesus said, "Your faith has made you whole," and other times when He healed everyone whether they had faith or not.

Experience in some gifts also builds faith for the distribution of others. While teaching and preaching on the gifts of the Spirit and the ministry of healing in Tblisi, Georgia (just south of Russia), a man stood up and carried his eight or nine year old boy to the front of the platform. I had not given an invitation for anyone to come forward, but he came and stood in front. I turned to my translator, Koté, and asked, "What is wrong with the boy? What does he want?" The translator told me, "This boy was born blind. Everyone in this church knows he is blind." The first thought that passed through my mind was, "This is going to either be really good, or this is going to be really bad!" The pastors and people at that meeting had heard the gospel preached about healing and the faith expectations were high. The second thought I had was the story of Ronnie Coyne—and faith rose up in my heart.

I laid my hands on both sides of the boy's head, with my thumbs over his eyes, just as I had heard my pastor and Ronnie

Coyne describe so many times. I commanded the eyes to be whole and eyesight to come. Immediately the boy opened his eyes, looked up, and then around the room, and began to point to the light fixtures hanging down from the ceiling. In his Georgian tongue he began to say loudly, "Lights, lights, lights!" and point to the fixtures. I didn't have time to interview the father or the boy. All I can say is pandemonium happened. People began to flood out of their seats and run to the front for prayer. I called out to the pastors to begin to minister to people and many were healed that night. It still stands as one of my greatest memories in decades of ministry adventures. It was a clear example, as I understand it, of the combination of the gift of special faith (I had no doubt God was going to heal this boy) and the gifts of healing.

Biblical Examples:

- Moses is healed of leprosy as a sign (Exodus 4:6-7).

- Naaman, an uncircumcised Syrian, is healed of leprosy by dipping seven times in a dirty river (2 Kings 5:14).

- Elijah raises the Shunammite's son from the dead (2 Kings 4:26-32).

- Jesus heals all that come to Him (Matthew 4:14; 8:16-17; 12:15; Luke 6:19).

- Paul heals everyone that was sick on the island of Malta (Acts 28:9)

- Paul raises Eutychus from the dead (Acts 20:9).

DISCUSSION QUESTIONS

1. How is the gift of faith different from the measure of faith that everyone possesses?

2. What is the difference between miracles and healings?

3. Tell a story of your own involvement in one of the Power gifts.

CHAPTER SIX

UTTERANCE GIFTS

PROPHECY

My wife and I were ministering at the altar after service, and a young couple came for prayer. We ministered to them, but the wife seemed "stuck." Then I saw a picture and knew it was for her. I described what I had seen: a little girl, dressed in a beautiful white frilly dress, with flowers around her head, swirling care-free and full of laughter. This young woman standing before me immediately started crying—deep sobs. She said, "How do you know that?" Then she explained that for some time she had been asking the Lord to show her how He sees her, and she would get a vision, but always thought it was her own imagination. But when I described the exact same picture, it was a confirmation to her, both that God indeed sees her that way, and that He loves her so much that He would use a stranger to confirm it through a prophetic word. She had a breakthrough and left the service encouraged, comforted, and with a new sense of identity and of God's love for her.

The gift of prophecy is defined as a supernatural utterance in a known tongue (known to the speaker and hearers), not conceived by human thought or reasoning, spoken by the inspiration of God to edify, encourage, strengthen, and comfort the church. Prophecy (and the utterance gifts), unlike the other manifestations of the Spirit, is given primarily to the Church for the purpose of encouraging and strengthening the Body of

it has been too easy for those who want to live within the confines of a safe and predictable, non-supernatural Christianity, to discard the gifts as self-centered extremism. Christ. The parameters are *"edification, exhortation and comfort"* (1 Corinthians 14:3), or as the English Standard Version says, "upbuilding and encouragement and consolation."

Since there are common misconceptions about New Testament prophecy, it is important to note what prophecy is not. It is not preaching (which can be generated strictly by human ability). Inspirational prophecy is not for guidance, direction or foretelling the future (though the encouragement may lift the eyes toward the future); it is more about edification than revelation. It is not a means for open rebuke or criticism. It is a supernatural impartation to the church to lift perspective, conduct, and faith. I will make a distinction later between inspirational prophecy and revelational prophecy—both may be considered an operation of this manifestation gift, but at different levels and for different reasons.

As in the operation of any of the utterance gifts, human agency can hinder its effectiveness, clarity, and accuracy. It can be personal (directed to an individual) but is not to be given privately (every word must be judged). Prophecy is speaking the mind or counsel of God, but only partially ("we prophesy in part" 1 Corinthians 13:9). In fact, all the utterance gifts are subject to (under the ultimate control of) the one speaking (1 Corinthians 14:32). We cannot cop out on our responsibility by saying, "I only say whatever I hear God say, you'll have to talk to him about it." No, you are responsible for every word you speak when prophesying, and your words need to be observed, evaluated and affirmed by other leaders in the church as being edifying and inspiring. If someone comes to you and wants to give you "a word", but they are unwilling to give that word in the presence of others, tell them, "Thanks, but no thanks."

Unfortunately, it has been too easy for those who want to live within the confines of a safe and predictable, non-supernatural

Christianity, to discard the gifts as self-centered extremism. But Paul makes it clear that spiritual gifts are one way God pours His love out to His Church. In addition, Paul says that among all of the manifestations of the Spirit, our top priority should be to prophesy. Notice this important statement from Paul, *"Pursue love, and earnestly desire the spiritual gifts, especially that you may prophesy"* (1 Corinthians 14:1, ESV). Love is the driving force of the gifts of the Spirit.

If you have been raised around those who disparage prophecy you should know that Paul spends significant time instructing the Corinthian believers about the priority of prophecy as a means of encouraging and strengthening fellow believers. Throughout this 14th chapter he contrasts the benefits of personal prayer language and the public function of tongues and interpretation of tongues as an equivalent function of prophecy that strengthens the whole church in love. Contrary to the way many commentators and pastors characterize this chapter, Paul never suggests that prophecy (or tongues for that matter) should be squelched. In fact, he finishes the chapter by re-emphasizing its importance again, *"So, my brothers, earnestly desire to prophesy, and do not forbid speaking in tongues"* (1 Corinthians 14:39).

Paul says, *"Now I want you all to speak in tongues, but even more to prophesy. The one who prophesies is greater than the one who speaks in tongues, unless someone interprets, so that the church may be built up"* (1 Corinthians 14:5). The one who speaks in a tongue builds up himself, but the one who prophesies builds up the church. The one who prophesies speaks to people for their upbuilding, encouragement, and consolation.

Note that the Bible says that *"all may prophesy"* (1 Corinthians 14:31), we are to *"covet to prophesy"* (1 Corinthians14:39), and we should *"despise not prophesying"* (1 Thessalonians 5:20). When a diversity of tongues are accompanied with interpretation of tongues, the complementary gifts equal prophecy (1 Corinthians 14:5).

Biblical Examples:

• When believers were filled with the Spirit in Luke's accounting in The Acts of the Apostles, they spoke with tongues and prophesied (Acts 19:6)

• We don't know exactly how the Holy Spirit spoke to the elders in Antioch but most likely it would have been a prophetic word through the prophets that were present (Acts 13:2-3).

• It wasn't rare in the early Church as it is today. The church norm was that everyone came with a tongue, a revelation, an interpretation (1 Corinthians. 14:26).

A NECESSARY DISTINCTION

Part of the problem that has given prophecy the bad rap is a lack of distinction between inspirational prophecy and revelational prophecy. Inspirational prophecy is what everyone can do—*"you may all prophesy"* (1 Corinthians14:31) and that kind of prophesying is to be positive and encouraging. Then there is a kind of prophesying which can include correction, judgment and may refer to revelational features that concern the future. This operation is given to the prophets as five-fold leaders of the Church (Ephesians 4:11-12). There is a different level of anointing and responsibility that is required of those who stand in the office of the prophet, and that which the common believer possesses. Much damage has been done when believers that should be ministering within the parameters of edification and encouragement try to move in revelational prophecy, touching on future events. Additionally, pastoral leaders that don't know the difference between revelational

...if pastoral leaders understand the things of the Spirit and teach their people its importance, the people will flourish as partners with the Holy Spirit.

and inspirational prophecy do their congregants a disservice. If we don't teach our people the difference we will subconsciously snuff out the operation of the gifts to avoid the messes that are produced by the lack of understanding and clarity. On the other hand, if pastoral leaders understand the things of the Spirit and teach their people its importance, the people will flourish as partners with the Holy Spirit.

Notice an interesting contrast in the Scriptures between the simple manifestation of inspirational prophecy and the office gift of revelational prophecy:

On the next day we departed and came to Caesarea, and we entered the house of Philip the evangelist, who was one of the seven, and stayed with him. He had four unmarried daughters, who prophesied. While we were staying for many days, a prophet named Agabus came down from Judea. And coming to us, he took Paul's belt and bound his own feet and hands and said, "Thus says the Holy Spirit, 'This is how the Jews at Jerusalem will bind the man who owns this belt and deliver him into the hands of the Gentiles'" (Acts 21:8-11).

Notice Philip's four daughters evidently functioned in the simple gift of inspirational prophesy. Perhaps there was a church that met at Philip's house (he would have been the natural leader) and the daughters would be known for their function in the house church. But when the prophet Agabus came down from Jerusalem, he operated in a higher level of gifting, in the office of the prophet, and the daughters were silent. Agabus' prophecy was not limited to edification, exhortation, and comfort. Rather, he spoke of the future and suffering that was to come to Paul. The distinction is important but should not hinder everyone from inspirational prophecy—compassion by the Spirit moves us to partner with Him to edify, exhort and comfort.

VARIOUS KINDS OF TONGUES

My father, Max Wood, was raised in a traditional Christian home with a good grasp of the Bible. He knew about the Father and Jesus, but heard precious little about the Holy Spirit—and certainly did not grow up hearing about His gifts. In fact, his college Bible teacher had explicitly stated that everything in the Book of Acts was only applicable to the first century Church. Then he met Mary, who would later become his wife. He says she was the most beautiful girl he had ever seen and was willing to do anything to win her friendship. When she invited him over for lunch before they even started dating he didn't realize this was something of an interview with her parents. Mary wasn't allowed to go out with guys that weren't Spirit-filled, much less "unsaved". During lunch, Mary's mom, Flora, asked Max if he knew Jesus. He said yes. Then she asked, "Have you met the Comforter?" (This was her favorite term to refer to the Holy Spirit). Max said he didn't, later confessing he didn't know what she was talking about. Then she said, "Mary will probably be inviting you to come to church with her." Of course he agreed under such circumstances.

It was a little Pentecostal church in Levelland, Texas. Though it was a new experience for him, Max was willing to do anything for her. Mary was concerned that the different style of worship would be too much for him. A little lady began to speak out a message in an unknown language. Mary tightened nervously and put her hand on Max's arm to settle him. He didn't move. On the way home from church Mary asked Max what he had thought of the service—and in particular about the message in tongues. "Was it weird?," she asked. "Not at all," Dad said. "It was unlike anything I have ever experienced, but when that lady began speaking in that language God started speaking just to me. He said, 'I want you to go deeper; I want you to know me better." When telling this story he always adds that this was the point in his life when he first began to really hunger for God. Now, at 84 years of age, his eyes well up with tears as he recalls God inviting him to get to know Him better. My dad has demonstrated to his family a long and steady walk in the fullness of the Holy Spirit. But he also raises question on the notion that a message in tongues automatically scares people.

I was baptized in the Holy Spirit at the age of nine and a feeble prayer language accompanied it. It wasn't a pretty language at first; more accurately described by Paul's reference to Isaiah 28:11 as "stammering lips." But it was not a strange or foreign thing to me—I heard people speaking in tongues practically every week at church and it didn't seem weird to me at all. It gave us the assurance of the presence of the Spirit among us. So a few years later, while I was singing a "special" (that's what we called the song between the regular hymn singing and the sermon), I began to notice something different. I felt my heart begin to race more than usual. While I was singing thoughts began to come to my mind beyond the lyrics, and with them a sense that I was to say something after the song was over. It was certainly a sense of impending inspiration.

As I concluded the song, I started speaking with a beyond-me kind of boldness in another language. I don't remember what the interpretation was. I only remember a sense of exhilaration swept across the congregation with audible responses of encouragement and joy. The Holy Spirit had done something through someone that energized the atmosphere for everyone else. It was an other-centered experience that felt like a mysterious partnership. And though praying in the Spirit was not new to me, this utterance came with a heightened intensity.

Any time we talk about the manifestation gift of "diverse kinds of tongues" we must spend some time clarifying the difference between tongues as a prayer language and tongues as a manifestation for the encouragement of the church.

The manifestation of diverse kinds of tongues or a diversity of tongues is a public supernatural utterance proclaiming the mind of the Spirit to a congregation or group in a language unknown to the speaker, and is to be exercised in conjunction with an interpretation into the known language.

It is a supernatural but temporary endowment having nothing to do with learned languages, a keen ability to learn languages, or the work of linguists. In other words, it is not a mental capability. It is the same in essence and function as the Spirit-filled believer's "prayer language," but different in purpose and use—one is speech directed to God (1 Corinthians 14:2), and the other is a manifestation that, accompanied with the interpretation of tongues, is intended to encourage the church, directed to people (14:3).

The manifestation of the Spirit sometimes called a "message in tongues" is not to be confused with the initial physical evidence of the baptism in the Holy Spirit. The gift of the Holy Spirit is more than tongues. He is a Person. When God wants to give you a gift, He sends a person. Many sincere believers get hung up on Spirit Baptism because they think they are trying to receive a language instead of the overflow of a Person.

The manifestation of diverse kinds of tongues can have two expressions. *Glossolalia* is a "strange" language that the person has not learned but is enabled to speak by the Holy Spirit. Paul refers to "tongues of men and of angels" in 1 Corinthians 13:1. *Xenoglossy (dialeipo)* is speaking of a human language (dialects) not known to the speaker, by the inspiration of the Holy Spirit (Acts 2: 5-6). In other words, someone hearing the message understands what is being said though the one speaking it does not understand. This was the case at Pentecost (Acts 2:8-12).

It seems that personal prayer language is the experiential on-ramp for all the other manifestation gifts of the Spirit. As we become comfortable partnering with the Spirit in private prayer, public expressions are not as tantalizing. Therefore, the likelihood that a person would be used to express this gift without first experiencing the initial physical evidence of the Baptism in the Holy Spirit is rare, though not inconceivable.

Biblical References:

- 1 Corinthians 14 is a complete instruction booklet on the proper management of the gifts of tongues and interpretation as prophecy so that the body may be edified and sinners convinced.

- Paul refers to Isaiah 28:11-12 as pertaining to the gift of a diversity of tongues.

- Other references to tongues (whether praying or singing) in the New Testament pertain to the believer's prayer language (Ephesians 5:19; 6:18; Colossians 3:16; Jude 20; 1 Corinthians 14:14, 15).

INTERPRETATION OF TONGUES

The manifestation gift of the interpretation of a message in tongues is a supernatural unfolding of the sense of a message given to a group or congregation in an unknown tongue so that the church may be encouraged and comforted. The basic idea of the work of the Spirit to interpret a tongue is to make an unintelligible message understandable. It is not a word-for-word translation of the tongue, but an interpretation of the sense or thrust of the Spirit's message. The interpreter does not understand the unknown tongue he/she is interpreting; it is not natural foreign language translation. Once a message in tongues is spoken out in a congregational setting, the operation of interpretation of tongues requires a measure of faith. For the interpreter, usually only enough thought or meaning is given by the Spirit to exercise a first step in faith. That may come as a picture, a word, a series of thoughts, or a general theme. Sometimes the Holy Spirit will take a thought from another area of study, perhaps from that morning's devotional time or something prompted by one of the worship songs form earlier in a service.

The highest principle in the operation of the gifts is love—in particular a love that is manifested in edification, exhortation, and comfort...

It is difficult to know with any certainty the context or the problems that Paul was dealing with in the Corinthian letter. It would be a mistake to make his regulations for their temporary problem (e.g. "two or three may speak in unknown tongues and one interpret"—1 Corinthians. 14:27), a permanent and universal litmus for the whole Church. Most Western churches are not facing the same problems the Corinthians faced. For example, Paul says to the Corinthian believers, *"You all come with a tongue, a revelation, a prophecy..."* (1 Corinthians 14:26). In other words, "when you guys come to church you come fully loaded and ready to minister to one another." But such is not generally the case in the twenty-first century church. Many attend church for years and never bring a message in tongues, a prophecy or a revelation. And, of course, Paul says to the Corinthians that "you all may prophesy" (14:31). So rather than apply a universal solution to every occasional problem, we draw the higher principle and apply the principle to our own similar problems. The highest principle in the operation of the gifts is love—in particular a love that is manifested in edification, exhortation, and comfort of the Church so that all are edified and matured.

Biblical References:

The Bible doesn't provide specific examples of a message in tongues and interpretation. We have examples of prophetic utterances, but it is not clear if these were direct prophesies, or tongues with interpretation, where the biblical author simply gives us the resulting prophetic insight. However, given Paul's admonition to the Corinthian church *"that two or three may speak in an unknown tongue and one interpret"* (1 Corinthians 14:27), it is clear that this was to be the norm in the gatherings of the Early Church.

DISCUSSION QUESTIONS

1. Why would Paul instruct us to prophesy with edification, exhortation and comfort and how does it reveal the nature of God?

2. What is the difference between revelational and inspirational prophecy?

3. If diverse kinds of tongues and interpretation are equal to prophecy, then why is tongues and interpretation of tongues needed at all?

CHAPTER SEVEN

PASTORAL CONSIDERATIONS

I developed a "pastoral sense" over a few decades of pastoral ministry that taught me to watch and listen for the Spirit's theme in a service. Sometimes that theme can be somewhat pre-orchestrated by wise pastoral and worship partnership in the prayerful planning so that a clear theme is seen in both the worship and teaching. My sense is that a team of leaders, when following the orchestration of the Spirit, will partner in the weaving of a thematic tapestry that reinforces one clear message to the congregation. I have also found that, just as often, the Spirit will spontaneously add a dimension to a prepared theme as a compassionate response to a need in the room. It is always an adventure to attempt to go with the flow of the "wind that blows wherever it wills."

All of that is to point to a certain guiding pastoral role in the gift of interpretation of a tongue. 1 Corinthians 12:27-28 indicates that the five-fold equipping gifts (Ephesians 4:11-12) also carry certain corresponding manifestation gifts—tools in the tool belt, so to speak. The apostle and evangelist needs the working of miracles and gifts of healings to confirm the word preached for the establishing of new churches. Prophets, of course, would function in heightened levels of the utterance gifts and revelation gifts. Pastors and teachers need administrative gifts to govern, but also the gifts of tongues and interpretation of tongues. And the reason for this is bound up in the practicality of love. Love insists on providing a safe place for disciples to grow and experiment in God.

If Paul says *"you may all prophesy"* (1 Corinthians 14:31) and tongues and interpretation of tongues is considered equal to prophecy in the function of bringing inspiration (1 Corinthians 14:5), then people need to be able to exercise those gifts for maturity. And most people will not take the risk to step out in faith and exercise a vocal gift unless they feel safe. A pastor needs to be able to provide a safe environment for people to grow and learn in the partnering with the Spirit for the edifying of the church without the fear of embarrassment or humiliation. How can a pastor provide a safe environment?

First, a pastor or leader must stay in tune with the Spirit personally so that he/she senses the direction of the Spirit. Secondly, a pastoral leader must be ready to function in the vocal gifts, especially in the operation of the interpretation of tongues. This is critically important so that believers know that there is an *"interpreter present"* (1 Corinthians 14:28), and with that knowledge feel the freedom and security to take steps of faith. Finally, pastors can minimize the impact of mistakes. If you are going to learn anything new you are going to make mistakes. Love covers mistakes. There have been numerous occasions in my pastoral ministry when a believer would give a message in an unknown tongue and no one would interpret. If I, as pastoral leader in that gathering, let that fall to the ground, I know the person who took that step of faith might be discouraged and never risk taking that step of partnership again. So I stay in sync with Holy Spirit and interpret that message in tongues. My desire is to let others in the congregation develop in those gifts. But if they don't speak up, I provide the safety for the congregation.

The negative side of that equation is also true. If someone the congregation doesn't know—a visitor for example—attempts to minister without relational equity, I provide protection there as well. I am not going to allow someone to come in and prophesy if we don't know them. 1 Thessalonians 5:12 says, "know those who labor among you," and I follow that as a general rule. I believe the Lord gifts pastoral leaders with the tools in their tool box to function in their office for the love and blessing of the people.

Remember, interpreters (those whom the Spirit tends to use) should be known to the church (1 Corinthians 14:28), and the gifts are inspired by the Spirit but administered by the Church (1 Corinthians 14:26-27).

PART III - GROWING IN THE GIFTS

CHAPTER EIGHT

HINDRANCES TO THE OPERATION OF THE GIFTS OF THE SPIRIT

"Spiritual Gifts are as optional as eyesight; you can walk without eyes, but you cannot see without them!"
—Harold Horton

I have had many conversations with pastoral leaders over the years from a variety of denominational and theological backgrounds. Many pastors have genuine hunger and sincere questions about a world they acknowledge knowing little about. Others stand guard over a doctrinal or denominational position which they feel is threatened by any focus on the Holy Spirit. One pastor was under the assumption that the absence of the gifts of the Spirit and healings in his church was solid evidence the days of miracles are over. He asked, "If the gifts are indeed in operation today, how come I don't see them in my church?" It is a good, valid question which merits thoughtful answers. And I would suggest up front that if we are not teaching our congregations that the Holy Spirit is still distributing gifts today, then congregants are neither expecting them nor considering the possibility. How different this is from Paul's admonition to "earnestly seek the best gifts."

...if we are not teaching our congregations that the Holy Spirit is still distributing gifts today, then congregants are neither expecting them nor considering the possibility.

I am offering some suggestions in this chapter as to why we don't see more the gifts of the Spirit in operation in our churches. Of course, my primary experience is in the Westernized culture of the United States—and all of these conditions are not the same in other countries and cultures. I readily acknowledge that there are other hindrances that could be articulated, but it is my experience that these are the predominant issues in my context. The first five hindrances are externals cultural hindrances (i.e. the effects of surrounding cultural and social environment). The remaining seven could be categorized as internal personal hindrances (i.e. things we believe and ways we think).

CHAPTER NINE

EXTERNAL CULTURAL HINDRANCES

1. AN ANTI-SUPERNATURAL WORLDVIEW

We don't realize it, but if we've been raised in the West we possess a prevailing Western Enlightenment, anti-supernatural mindset—an unconscious bias against the reality of the spirit world.

Physicists are spending billions to build atomic super-colliders in hopes of discovering the parallel universe (i.e. the spirit world) that they refuse to believe exists—unless, of course, they can verify it by empirical scientific method. Man is too smart for God and will build his tower to the heavens. It reminds me of the story of the scientific expedition where the elite intellectuals scaled the highest peak of human knowledge. And when they pulled themselves up to the edge of the precipice and peeked over to catch the first glimpse of the heavenly summit—there was a group of theologians sitting around a campfire talking to God. Honest science will always eventually verify Truth as revealed in Scripture—but not all science is honest presently—there are many agendas.

Unfortunately, this empirically driven worldview has seeped into the Church. Modern systematic theology with all its higher criticism has "taken the bait" from the world's system to prove scientifically what is not, cannot, and never will be subject to the sciences that are limited to only the natural/physical part of God's world. God's universe is a holistic one that encompasses dimensions the fallen natural man cannot see and cannot study...

"The natural person does not accept the things of the Spirit of God, for they are folly to him, and he is not able to understand them because they are spiritually discerned" (1 Corinthians 2:14).

It is important for the modern/post-modern believer, especially the new generation believer to understand that if you have grown up in the West, you are a fish who has never known any water but the worship of modern science. We don't even realize the degree to which all our cultural mindsets have been "set to default" on an anti-supernatural view. We have watched, from Scooby Doo to CSI, Hollywood's de-spiritualization of reality. What starts out looking like a spiritual mystery is decoded within twenty-three minutes (plus commercials) to nothing more than an uncanny conglomeration of natural coincidences. And yet the internal spiritual longing persists within the human breast.

Is this not the perfect time for a new generation to begin living beyond the limitations of the natural barriers of a failed science? Is not post-modernity ripe for a sweeping exposure into the life beyond life? Who will carry the torch to this generation to expose the invisible world as the good creation of a God who longs to be discovered as the overflowing love that He is? Perhaps people moving in the gifts of the Spirit would dislodge the world from its moorings enough so God could coax us into the parallel universe called the Kingdom of God.

2. Poor Teaching

Many believers have been raised up under either poor teaching, no teaching or antagonistic teaching about the things of the Spirit. Erroneous teaching in the Church has been a huge hindrance. The most influential heresy of modern times is the notion that the gifts of the Spirit have passed away or are not necessary for today's organized church.

Carroll Thompson,[5] pastor and missionary evangelist, tells of his need for a lifestyle that embraces the fullness of the Holy Spirit and all of His gifts. Carroll began preaching at the age of 19, and pastoring shortly thereafter. He attended a prominent seminary of a denomination which taught that the "gifts of the Spirit" were given by God for the birthing and launching of the Church, but not necessary for today. After seminary he went to Brazil as a missionary, not knowing the reality of the spirit dimension that awaited him. He had never seen demonic manifestations and transparent spiritual warfare as was the norm in Latin American syncretistic Catholicism. He had never seen such in the United States and it was easy to simply ignore it. He started his ministry in Brazil full of zeal, putting into practice everything that he had learned in seminary and teaching the mantra of his teachers, that the gifts had ceased—until he was confronted with evil spirits. Carroll realized that all of his training and knowledge of Scripture was not enough to win this battle. When he was stricken with a life-threatening disease, he cried out to the Lord saying, "I can't handle this! I need Your help!" He experienced a supernatural visitation, and Jesus baptized him in the Holy Spirit and healed him. This experience unleashed a new dimension in Carroll's ministry, with an abundance of manifestations of the gifts of the Spirit. When his denomination heard of his experience and the miracles that were manifesting among the churches, they dismissed him. But Carroll, full of the Holy Spirit, has continued in supernatural ministry for more than 60 years.

Carroll Thompson's story is not an isolated one. That reality has been repeated so many times over the past thirty to forty years that the Southern Baptist Convention announced this week (the week of this writing), that it has changed its position on Spirit Baptism for its missionaries.[6] Some still can't bring themselves to acknowledge that the spiritual reality of darkness versus light exists in all countries and cultures.

3. Ignoring the Holy Spirit

A lack of teaching about the Holy Spirit has cultivated a willingness to ignore the Holy Spirit and His desire to heal, mend and bless through the Church. A huge hindrance to functioning in the gifts of the Spirit is simply ignoring the Holy Spirit as the ready and willing initiator of a supernatural supply. The new languaging of the social sciences and humanities was shaped by psychology and blended with North American notions of success, which served to keep the focus on the felt needs of people in the pew, rather than broadcasting healing and wholeness to the world. At the same time, our general prosperity made it easier for those needing healing to run first to the doctor. For those needing direction, there's a "life coach," and for those struggling with depression there is a world of psychiatrists with a smorgasbord of therapies available. But where these option aren't as plentiful, people are more ready to call on God and expect the answer from Him.

My grandmother, Flora Massey, was raised very poor and lived on modest (i.e. meager) means all her life. She came to understand very early that God was her only option for most necessities in life. Subsequently, she learned to fast and pray and believe God for healings, answers to prayer and miracles. Going to a hospital was the farthest thing from her mind, even in the case of extreme sickness. She told me on more than one occasion that if she ever got sick she would "drink a glass of hot lemon water" and if that didn't take care of it, she would lock herself in the bathroom and fast and pray until she was healed. She trusted God with her life. At almost 100 years of age, her neighbors found her with a broken hip—she was believing God for healing. They called '9-1-1' and she was taken to the hospital with no questions asked. Needless to say, she was not happy with her neighbors! At that time she was the oldest person to undergo hip replacement surgery. A couple of weeks later she was on the exercise bike in the therapy ward, with doctors and nurses standing in amazement as she exercised and sang hymns at the top of her lovely but warbley voice. She died a week short of completing her 106th year, sitting in her letter-writing chair, praying in the Spirit.

He wants mankind to see how good and faithful our Father really is.

Do we have to be poor to rely on the Holy Spirit? No. We can learn to put the Spirit first in our lives, no matter how many comforts, conveniences or medical innovations are available to us. Yes, God's healing also happens through the medical profession, for which we are grateful—but our reliance on the Holy Spirit is to never be replaced by natural means. He wants mankind to see how good and faithful our Father really is.

In the past century, much of the Church worldwide made considerable progress to acknowledge the Holy Spirit. Vinson Synan named the 20th century the "Century of the Holy Spirit." But in the West He is still the "it", the mystical unknown, the strange uncle at the family reunion. He's been called "the forgotten member of the Trinity" and "the God I never knew."[7] There is no question that some excesses within the Pentecostal movement in its early days contributed to the mainline denominations keeping some distance, or even castigating the Pentecostals as heretics. But the Charismatic movement of the 1970's and 1980's exposed enough of a cross-section of the Western Church to what God was doing in the rest of the world, that more objectivity began to get a foothold in the broader theology. For this, I am grateful, but there remains much work to be done to introduce Holy Spirit as the God who is with us and for us.

4. Lack of Leadership

A lack of modeling of the operation of the gifts of the Spirit has proven to be a huge hindrance to the Church's being equipped to do the work of the ministry (Eph 4:10, 11). There is no intent to cast dispersion upon church leaders. I am a church leader, and have been one long enough that I must bear my share of responsibility for where the Church currently stands in both understanding and fruitfulness, or the lack thereof. The fact is, we all learn best by watching others do what we cannot do. This is true of children and adults. What church leaders do (in contrast to what leaders say) sends the clearest signal of what church leaders deem most important. If prayer is important the congregation will not only be called to pray regularly, but will learn to pray by watching and hearing our leaders pray. Dr. Paul (David) Yonggi Cho, pastor of the world's largest church at the end of the Twentieth century, regularly asserted that churches that pray are led by pastors who lead the prayer meetings.

Likewise, if the gifts of the Spirit are never modeled in front of the congregation, how will believers know of its importance or normalcy? What is "normal" is what leaders do in front of us, and what is not normal (i.e. "weird") is whatever leaders don't do in front of us. This is influence; this is leadership.

In the section on "Getting to Know the Gifts," I tell the story of my childhood exposures to the things of the Spirit. It made all the difference for me in moving forward in the partnership of the Spirit. That is not to say I have done it all right or that I don't have a long way to go yet. The church my family attended during my childhood years was committed to life in the Spirit. I was reared in churches that lived and breathed prayer. I heard stories constantly and saw miracles and healings enough to know that it was more than biblical history.

My firsthand exposure to Kathryn Kuhlman's ministry and Ronnie Coyne's ongoing miracle, plus almost weekly healings in our church and the resulting testimonies, deeply rooted me into a belief system that the days of healings, miracles and the gifts of the Spirit are not over. Even as an eleven-year-old I was acclimated to the miraculous through my 5th grade Sunday School teacher, J. C. Evans. He was a man's man, an oilfield roughneck from Odessa, Texas. He would tell stories almost every Sunday of how God spared his life from a rig accident or how he ministered to some belligerent God-hater. With hands that were missing two or three fingers and tears running down his face, he would keep my fifth grade buddies and me on the edge of our seats. We would come to class asking, "What has God done for Brother Evans this week?" I was cultivated with a hunger for a life in God. And it was exactly because of that exposure to the supernatural that I became somewhat frustrated a few years later, with a powerless Church that loved to talk and sing about God's miraculous deeds, but didn't seem to care to see it for themselves. And that exposure compelled me to gravitate toward those who were willing to take the risks of faith. I wonder what it will take to ignite a new generation to the realm of God?

5. LACK OF HUNGER

A lack of spiritual hunger for the Supernatural in the Church begets generations that don't know their own spiritual heritage nor the power of God. As the Church has become more and more dependent on technology, and driven by a compulsion to stay cutting edge, it has also reaped a few not-so-beneficial results such as time-constraints imposed by television production (e.g. length of service due to multi-media recordings, etc.) such that the practicalities of spontaneity are minimized for sake of professionalism and efficiency. I thoroughly understand that many of the things of the Spirit don't translate well on national television or even video clips on YouTube! What can seem perfectly natural and spontaneous in person may look bizarre and fanatical on camera. And how the naysayers love to edit those clips together and make free and whole-hearted worshippers look unhinged.

I find that spiritual hunger takes time. Fasting and prayer are not on the take-out menu, nor can they be downloaded by 4G, 5G or whatever comes after 6G speed. Spiritual hunger is totally counter-intuitive to this generation's cultural pace, but God does not pass out the secrets of His heart to casual

God does not pass out the secrets of His heart to casual seekers. He longs for intimacy, and intimacy takes time.

seekers. He longs for intimacy, and intimacy takes time.

The Lord anchored this truth home to me during my first pastorate. We were having special meetings and I was asking the Lord do something significant in the church. But most of my congregation were farmers and I was mindful that they had to arise before dawn to care for their animals and ranching duties. During the first night, the service was going much longer than planned and I was getting stressed out "for our folks." When the guest speaker finally gave an invitation for personal ministry, it was so late in the evening that I was sure no one would be interested in receiving prayer and I was agitated.

I thought we had missed it, but to my surprise almost ninety-percent of the crowd responded to the speaker's invitation, stepped out of their seats and headed to the front. I couldn't believe it! And then I heard the Lord say, "Kerry, that's your problem. You don't give Me a chance to work in people. You're in too big of a hurry."

That wasn't a fun lesson, but the Lord reinforced to me what I should have already known; spiritual hunger takes time. When I reflect back on my childhood I realize that my own spiritual hunger was developed in seasons of seeking God. We spent time around the front of the church both before and after the services praying, listening, singing and waiting.

My dad tells about when he became so hungry for the fullness of the Spirit that he told God, "I'm not going to eat again until I receive all You have for me!" He was filled with the Spirit that week. And you may have heard of the Hebrides Revival, where two ladies in their 80's, prayed for revival from 10:00 in the evening until 3:00 or 4:00 in the morning, two days each week for months. God heard their cry and history records that God swept in by His power and brought revival over the Scottish Islands that lasted more than three years.

Why does God insist that we wait on Him, hunger after Him and cry out to Him? Is there something lacking in Him that He needs earthlings to need Him? No, He needs nothing. But He wants us to know that He is the only true source for life and love.

Knowledge from the tree won't fill us. Positions, possessions or power won't fill us. He is our only source and He has made us to be filled only by His love.

I love a song that we are singing right now that simply says, "Were waiting here for You." The more we give ourselves to seeking God, the more spiritual hunger will be developed in our souls. Draw near to God and He will draw near to you.

DISCUSSION QUESTIONS

1. Which of the "external hindrances" is having the greatest negative impact on the Church in your own culture?

2. If we live in a measure of affluence and an anti-supernatural worldview how can hunger for God be cultivated?

3. In which of these areas do you feel the Lord has spoken to you personally?

CHAPTER TEN

INTERNAL PERSONAL HINDRANCES

6. SENSE OF INADEQUACY

The gifts of the Spirit are the primary way the Holy Spirit draws us into a partnership into the life and mission of God. It is the indwelling Holy Spirit who enables us to do what we could never do on our own. And yet, so many are bound with a sense of inadequacy that makes the things of the Spirit seem like a fairy tale. We can believe that He gives gifts of healings through some great men and women of God, but the enemy makes sure we quickly follow that acknowledgment with "but who am I to think God would use me in those supernatural ways?"

Two weeks ago I was talking to someone who had attended the class I was teaching that morning. I had been talking about how God has made us in His image and desires to bring us into partnership in mission so we can enjoy life as God has it. This friend reported a conversation they had just had with someone who sat in the class for the first time. When asked how they liked the class this person said, "Yes, it was great! But, do you believe what He was teaching is real? Do you believe that we can really know God like that and partner with Him?"

It shocks me to discover so many in the Church today that still feel so far from any kind of real life in God. Do we not know that we can lay hands on the sick and they will recover? Do we not

Praying in the Spirit and meditating upon the Words of God uproot a spirit of timidity and fear... know that the Holy Spirit lives in us and wants to have conversations with us daily about the things Father and Jesus are saying and doing? Have we not grasped that heaven is not just "out there" somewhere, in the sweet by and by, but we are making heaven available now—at least as a down payment on what will be? How has the Church, with so many teachers, Bibles and cutting-edge technologies, not grasped the significance of our sonship as the pivotal plot for planet earth? And how do we rationalize having the creative Spirit of God in us and yet not draw upon that reservoir of infinite resource via spiritual prayer in such a way as to have the supernatural advantage in every situation? Let me say it in the affirmative. The awareness of your sonship, and the reality of the indwelling Holy Spirit that makes sonship resources available, gives you the supernatural advantage in every situation.

7. Fear

This refers to the self-conscious focus that floods the mind with "what if's" -- what if nothing happens, what if I miss it? What if I give them this word and it doesn't mean anything to them? The devil loves to play us into the paralysis of analysis. Meanwhile, the Holy Spirit gives us boldness, empowering us to do what the Father says. We have not been given a spirit of timidity or fear, but power, love and a sound mind [clear thinking] (2 Timothy 1:7). Praying in the Spirit and meditating upon the Words of God uproot a spirit of timidity and fear so that we are willing to take faith-risks and carry the gifts from the Father to a broken world.

What If We Fail?

There are such things as "faith failures" though we don't like to talk about them. But contrary to common notions, even if we fail God is not going to point a stern, disapproving finger to say, "I am so disappointed in you. I raised you better than that. I can't trust you to do anything right." Even if you may have heard that from a parent, you will not hear that from Abba. The Lord will encourage you even if you make a mistake. This is why we have been given parameters and pointers in the operation of the gifts of the Spirit.

Paul tells the Corinthians to have a sense of order in the operation of the gifts and let the prophets-elders judge. This "judgement" is not so the well-meaning believer that says something wrong gets chastised in front of the congregation; just the opposite. Wise and loving pastoral leaders don't demean or humiliate people of their flock in front of the congregation—they talk to them privately to counsel, instruct and encourage them.

Paul tells the Corinthians that "all may prophesy" but that this kind of inspirational prophecy needs to be done in a way that "edifies, exhorts and comforts" (1 Corinthians 14:3). Why the parameters? Because if a person will partner with Holy Spirit in a way that will bless people, encourage and comfort them, most likely that word will minister blessing and encouragement even if it is not perfectly accurate. This is why we must see the gifts of the Spirit as they are, an overflow of God's infinite love and compassion, not an exercise in perfection.

I have come to the conclusion that most pastors don't allow room for the gifts to operate in their congregations because (1) they don't have much experience in the gifts themselves and feel incompetent to pastor these manifestations, (2) their lack of experience in the gifts produces an insecurity in themselves, and (3) the insecure leader is concerned about what people will think of his/her leadership if someone "messes up" in the partnership of the gifts of the Spirit. So we might think, "let's not risk failure."

My wife tells a story of learning to step out in partnership with Holy Spirit and battling the fear of failure. She says:

> There was a season in my life where I rode a bus to and from work every day. This was a comfortable bus ride from Sugar Land to the Galleria area in Houston, making only a few stops at a few office buildings in the Galleria, where I worked at the time. My custom was to use the time on the bus to pray and read my Bible. On one particular day I was having a conversation with the Lord, asking Him to use me as a conduit of His gifts. Though I had been exposed to the miraculous, I didn't have much experience with partnering with God in ministry. But I was hungry to see the supernatural in my life. I remember telling Him, "Just give me an opportunity to minister to someone. Whatever You ask of me, I will do it." Then I looked over, and on the other side of the bus was a lady with a neck brace. I sensed Holy Spirit saying, "Go and minister healing to her." Then the wrestling started. "What? Now? But she's reading her book." The lady put her book down. Holy Spirit said, "Now." I proceeded to argue some more. "But the bus is moving. It's not safe. What if nothing happens? What if...?" Holy Spirit said, "Weren't you just asking me to use you? Didn't you just say that if I asked you to do something, you would do it?" "Yes, but..." (When we are afraid to fail, it is easy to come up with excuses for why we can't do what God is asking us to do).
>
> Finally, on the stop before mine, I mustered up the courage to talk to her. I got up from my seat and went to the seat directly behind her, put my hand on her shoulder, and said, "Excuse me, would you mind telling me what is wrong with your neck?" She explained that she had some degeneration of the cervical vertebrae, and the neck brace was the doctor's attempt at slowing down the progression of this disease. I explained to her that I believed God wanted to do something in her life and

asked if she would mind if I prayed for her. Immediately, tears ran down her cheeks. She accepted. I prayed. I spoke healing over her. I expected to see a supernatural manifestation—one of those miracles that I had read about, where people experience intense heat, take off their braces and go running off, shouting "Hallelujah!" But none of that happened. The bus rolled to the stop, and I got off, feeling like a failure. And I talked about it to the Lord, feeling that He had set me up to fail. Why would He prompt me to go and do something like that? I felt so foolish! To make matters worse, this lady got off on the same stop. I didn't know that we worked in the same office building.

For the next three or four days, I avoided her! In the afternoon, before taking the bus back home, I would see if she was waiting for the same bus; and if she was, I would run back to my office and work an additional 20 minutes until the next bus. I didn't want to have to face her. She was a reminder of my ministry failure.

Then on Friday I was waiting for the bus, and out of nowhere, I see the same lady coming toward me saying, "I'm so glad to finally see you! I've been wanting to tell you..." She was still wearing her neck brace. What could she possibly want to tell me? It was too late to hide or to ignore her so I quietly listened as she told me her story. "I was raised in church," she said, "and I've always had a relationship with Jesus. But the last few months have been very difficult. And last week my cat died, and that was 'the last straw.' I became very depressed, and I was thinking that God had forgotten about me. And then you came over, and said that God had spoken to you about me, and that you wanted to pray for me. And right then I knew that God hadn't forgotten about me, and that He loves me. So I want to thank you for doing that!"

Now I was the one with tears running down my cheeks. What I had seen as a failure, was a significant moment for

Carol (I finally found out her name that day). I didn't see what I expected to see, but God was at work, and she felt His compassion through me.

If our expectation in the ministry of the gifts of the Spirit is for God to always work a certain way, heal the person on the spot every time, we will certainly fail (in our own eyes). But if we minister God's compassion to people, we can't fail. We may have expectations for what success looks like, but if we leave the details up to Him, He will receive the glory. He knows what He is doing. The burden is not on us to perform. If we will be willing to partner with God, reach out to others, and let them know His love, He will be faithful to confirm that message. He wants to restore a broken world, and He has called you—and me—to be overflowing carriers of His gifts so we can experience the joy of partnership with Him. The only real failure in the gifts is to either refuse to obey in sharing with others or to minister the gifts in a non-compassionate way.

8. MISTAKEN IDEAS OF "THE MINISTRY"

Another reason we hesitate to pursue the gifts of the Spirit is that we assume that God has chosen "ministers" (pastors, preachers, teachers) to do the miraculous works, but fail to realize those "ministry gifts" of Christ, mentioned in Ephesians 4:11-12, are for the equipping of the saints precisely so that the saints will do the work of ministry. These are none other than the works of Christ that Jesus spoke of in John 14:12-14, *"These same works (that I have done) you will do, and greater works than these will you do."* It is certainly true that Jesus gives gifts to five-fold leaders; but He never withdraws the responsibility of partnership with the Spirit to provide gifts to the Body. The five-fold leaders are

I wonder if we could change the mindset of the Church by training and treating every believer as a minister of the Gospel.

given to the Church so the Church will be equipped to do the ministry, not to sit back and watch the leaders do the ministry.

I wonder if we could change the mindset of the Church by training and treating every believer as a minister of the Gospel. What would that look like? I wonder if we could change our own mindsets by providing the same leadership training for the congregation as we do for the pastors. Whatever the method, we must never give in to the Old Testament notion that there is a priesthood that must do the work of the ministry on behalf of the people. He has made us all priests and kings.

9. LACK OF CULTIVATION

Life in the Spirit must be cultivated in one's personal life. Many have not cultivated a lifestyle of Spirit-fullness and subsequently, the things of God and the spirit-dimension itself seem remote. The Scriptures admonish, *"Mind the things of the Spirit"* (Romans 8:5). This is more than a suggestion to wholesome conduct or advancing good morals. Minding the things of the Spirit means to learn to live out of one's spirit (*pneuma*), build up the spirit man (Jude 20) and function as a citizen and player in the spirit dimension by the indwelling Holy Spirit, where spiritual warfare is constant and eternal harvest is contested.

We have effectively "dummied down" spirituality to a five-minute Bible reading in the morning and church attendance two or three Sundays each month. But no one can survive on one sip of water each morning and a small snack each weekend. Someone has said, *"The North American Christian is the only mammal on the planet that doesn't learn to feed himself within the first year of life."* That may sound harsh, but the net result is that many believers don't even think about God or "life in the Spirit" unless they are having their quiet time in the morning (and who said it's supposed to be quiet?) or at church on the weekend.

Paul said, *"I thank my God that I speak in tongues more*

than you all" (1 Corinthians 14:18). Why would he say this? Is it arrogance? Is it false spirituality? Especially in the context of the Corinthians' "excesses" of spiritual language in the assembly, why would he say such a thing? It is neither ignorance nor pride that motivates this statement. He is relating the inward empowerment of the Holy Spirit that comes by spiritual language (1 Corinthians 14:2-4) as the key to his ability to endure the incredible assaults he was experiencing in his ministry. But this is not just for the professionals; we are all called into the fight; so all must suit up for the spiritual warfare that is the call of the Church. Each one must put on the whole armor of God by praying in the Holy Spirit (Ephesians 6:18). But it must also be said that since you are reading about the gifts of the Spirit you are probably not a part of the spiritually lethargic crowd. You are clearly investing the extra time and energy to cultivate this life of the Spirit, which will pay huge dividends -- especially for many who need what you carry.

10. LACK OF INTENTIONALITY

There must be intentionality—even a contending for the things of the Spirit. For many believers this issue of hindrances to the gifts of the Spirit simply boils down to lack of intentionality; lacking a goal, a clear focus or a sense of mission. Paul said, *"Covet (earnestly desire and seek) the best gifts"* (1 Corinthians 14:1). Our attention often gets drawn to "the best gifts" and we lose sight of the fact that Paul calls for each of us to maintain a strong desire, even a coveting of partnership with Holy Spirit.

Perhaps these other hindrances have blinded us to the fact that Holy Spirit wants to partner with us for the Father's purposes. Perhaps we have bought into a subtle notion of a "works mentality" on one end or "nothing required" mindset on the other. But Jesus clearly said the He would send the Holy Spirit and, because of Him, *"the same works I have done you will do, and greater works than these you will do..."* (John 14:12).

We should be aware that Jesus did His works by the indwelling fullness and subsequent power of the Holy Spirit (Acts 10:38) and He has sent the same Holy Spirit into us that we might do the same works—multiplied by hundreds of millions of believers' faithfully partnering with the Spirit around the world.

11. Sin Consciousness

A major factor in the mindsets of would-be champions of God's works is an inward awareness of our past sins and/or present powerlessness. This has changed considerably in the past 40 to 50 years through an abundance of biblical teaching about "Who we are in Christ," the righteousness of God and the authority of the believer. The Church is better trained to use Jesus' name and stand in His promises than she has ever been. With that being said, there remain huge pockets of "deficit mindedness" in the Church—people who are more focused on where they have been than where they are going, what they have done rather than what they are doing. This is Satan's ploy, of course. If he can keep a believer thinking that he "will always be a sinner" and will never have true freedom from the old ways of sin and sinful habits, then that believer will be subject to the oppression of guilt and inadequacy. Guilt robs believers of boldness.

On the other hand, when a person stays full of the Spirit, part of the effects of that fullness is power and boldness. Jesus said, *"[When the Holy Spirit is come] you will be endued with power from on high"* (Acts 1:8). Later, Luke records the fulfillment of this promise: *"...and they were filled with the Holy Spirit and spoke the word of God with boldness"* (Acts 4:31). One of the great internal works of the indwelling Holy Spirit in preparing believers for the operation of the gifts is to free them from the power of sin and give them a sense of mastery over

...when a person stays full of the Spirit, part of the effects of that fullness is power and boldness.

sin in their lives (Romans 6:14).

12. UNCONFESSED SIN

Finally, it must be said that unconfessed sin is the "super-hindrance" to operating in the gifts of the Spirit. It does not mean that a person living in sin cannot experience the Holy Spirit, or even be used at times by the Holy Spirit. We would probably prefer that the Holy Spirit would not use someone who is living in sin—but the reality is that He operates through people "as He wills" (not as we will), and He has been known to use some scoundrels at times. Most could tell a story or two about a preacher-gone-wrong who has learned how to partner with Holy Spirit and becomes a charlatan and takes advantage of people. I can't say that I know in every case why the Holy Spirit keeps working through those people, but the evidence seems to show that His overflowing compassion moves Him to bless and heal even through imperfect vessels. But Samson is given as example that this doesn't last very long. The Holy Spirit will not be mocked.

My admonition to you would be the same as Peter's to Simon the sorcery, *"This power can't be bought with money; you will have to repent"* (paraphrase of Acts 8:20-23). God doesn't need false advertising; He can find enough pure hearts who seek after Him to do His work. His eyes run to and fro throughout the whole earth to show Himself strong on behalf of those whose hearts are right before Him.

Prayer

Do any of these "hindrances" resonate with you and where you are currently? Would you want to stop right now and ask, "Father, is there anything in any of these 12 hindrances that you would want to talk to me about? I'm going to get quiet and listen for Your voice as I look back over these.

Thank you, Father. I thank you for the Holy Spirit inside of me who strengthens me and equips me to see Your name glorified and broken people set free. I thank You that by the indwelling Holy Spirit I come behind in no gifts, but am enriched with every kind of knowledge and all divinely inspired speech, and lack nothing that would be needed to help and bless others (1 Corinthians 1:5-7).

Discussion Questions

1. Which of the "internal hindrances" do you struggle with more than others?

2. In what ways could we better prepare the Church to do the ministry as a gift-giving people?

3. Is there a significant hindrance that is missing in this list?

CHAPTER ELEVEN

WAYS TO CULTIVATE THE GIFTS, PART 1

I never get out of bed in the morning without having communion with God in the Spirit.
—Smith Wigglesworth

Do not neglect the gift that is in you, which was given to you by prophecy with the laying on of the hands of the eldership (1 Timothy 4:14).

Therefore I remind you to stir up the gift of God which is in you through the laying on of my hands (2 Timothy 1:6).

So with yourselves, since you are eager for manifestations of the Spirit, strive to excel in building up the church (1 Corinthians 14:12).

Paul concludes his admonition to the Corinthians about the gifts in 1 Corinthians 14:39-40 saying, "So, my brothers, earnestly desire to prophesy, and do not forbid speaking in tongues. But all things should be done decently and in order." We have emphasized the *"decently and in order"* and discarded the *"all things should be done"* (i.e. prophesying and speaking in tongues).

...we are spiritual beings wired for spiritual experience and supernatural ministry. If you did not grow up around the manifestations of the Spirit, you may face what seems like a vast chasm between "the way you were raised" and what you long for as a supernatural life in God. I will be first to admit that I have grown up around people who are more comfortable with the manifestations of the Holy Spirit than many Christians in the West. I was raised in churches of the largest Pentecostal denomination in North America. In those days most of these churches were passionate about the "manifest presence of God." Some of them remain this way while other have re-directed their focus. Yet I am constantly surrounded by believers that express a strong desire to be used of God in ministry that would involve the gifts of the Spirit.

The reality is, we are spiritual beings wired for spiritual experience and supernatural ministry. We read the stories of God's miraculous power to heal, rescue and restore people. Most believers can recite the stories of Jesus' healings and miracles— and it lodges in their own souls as something of which they are made to participate. *"These works that I do shall you do, and greater works than these will you do, because I go to My Father"* (John 14:12-14). Though many Christians will struggle with the dichotomy between Jesus' extraordinarily supernatural life and their own, there is a yearning to experience the reality of the early Church.

Like a new exercise regimen or the first paragraph of a research paper, it seems the hardest part of operating in the gifts of the Spirit is knowing how to get started. Perhaps this is why Paul reminded Timothy to "stir up the gift of God which is in you..." and to the Corinthians he said, "Desire the best gifts." But how does one stir up the gift? Consider some simple first steps.

Covet (Ardently Desire, Earnestly Seek) the Gifts

The first step in your quest to partner with God is to simply **start asking God to use you in supernatural ways** (1 Corinthians 12:31). Earnestly desire, ardently seek the best gifts. Various renderings of 1 Corinthians 12:31 say, *"Now eagerly desire the greater gifts"* (NIV), *"Pursue the greater gifts"* (The Voice), *"...earnestly desire and zealously cultivate"* (Amp), and *"You should set your hearts on the highest spiritual gifts"* (JB Philips). This seems strange because the gifts of the Spirit have been portrayed so often in a negative light. As we explained earlier, if we misunderstand God's nature, we will misunderstand the purpose and operation of the gifts, and consequently, it would seem that earnestly desiring gifts would be self-promoting. But, when we understand that the gifts are God's vehicles to restore the broken, we can covet the gifts to give them away in partnership with God, making His compassion known to a hurting world.

If a believer lives out of an orphan spirit, the gifts become a way to try to prove he is somebody—to validate his spirituality. The gifts then become a tool for self-promotion rather than an overflow of blessing from the Father's heart. Well-meaning believers, still living in an orphan spirit, grasping for a sense of identity and purpose, use the gifts of the Spirit as a means to prove their value and worth, and they cannot help but abuse the gifts and people in that process.

The reality is, we cannot simply choose to know we've been made worthy. This is a progressive work of the Holy Spirit in each believer's life and is more about heart transformation than head information. Most Christians have heard sermons and teachings about "who they are in Christ" but too often it hasn't uprooted the deep-seated lies they have believed about themselves. This is because the orphan spirit cannot

...when we understand that the gifts are God's vehicles to restore the broken, we can covet the gifts to give them away in partnership with God...

be taught out or preached out; it comes by displacement through revelation. The orphan script that plays in one's mind is one of failure, detachment from God, that there is always something more "out there" that is needed to be enough, do enough, and know enough. But the primary role of the indwelling Holy Spirit is to convince every believer of his or her "sonship" (Romans 8:14). The Holy Spirit is sent to convict and convince us of the reality that we are sons of God (John 16:8, 10; Galatians 4:1-4). Though a thorough treatment of the battle between a *spirit of sonship* and the orphan spirit is outside the primary scope of this book, it is critical to every believer's confidence in order to partner with Holy Spirit via the operation of the gifts.

The gifts of the Spirit are an overflow of God's other-centered love and compassion. It is out of the fullness of Who He is that He keeps giving Himself away—and every manifestation of the Spirit (1 Corinthians 12), every motivational gift (Romans. 12) and every leadership gift (Ephesians 4) is for healing, strengthening and restoring broken and wounded people. Is this what your heart longs for? Do you want to see the purposes of God in your own life? Do you want to be able tell the testimonies of God's wonderful works to your own children and grandchildren? Start asking God every day to use you. "Father, I make myself available today. I desire to partner with You. Speak to me, give me a gift to give away today. I desire the gifts that are most needed for the moment to be a blessing to someone else."

This passionate pursuit of a life in God, a more powerful existence, is born of a holy dissatisfaction with the status quo. It requires one to resist to allure of comfort and the gravitational pull of "the way it's always been." Lean into the discomfort of transformation. Begin to cry out to God to use you. Know that you have been made worthy by the blood of the Lamb and God desires your partnership. *"Call to Me, and I will answer you, and show you great and mighty things, which you do not know"* (Jeremiah 33:3).

PRAY IN THE SPIRIT AS A DISCIPLINE

Do you want to hear what is popular, or do you want to know the truth? The truth is, although most of the gifts of the Spirit do not require spiritual language,[8] praying in the Spirit has enormous personal benefits for those who desire to partner with the Spirit.

First, praying in the Spirit as a daily discipline is the best way to get comfortable working with Holy Spirit as partner. When a man prays in an unknown tongue his spirit prays by partnership with the Holy Spirit (1 Corinthians 14:2-4). The more a person prays in the Spirit and makes that a regular part of her personal life, the more normative the gifts of the Spirit will be and the more she will see life as naturally supernatural.

Second, operating in the gifts of the Spirit requires faith, and praying in the Spirit builds you up on your faith (Jude 20). What does this "built up faith" feel like? A person who is built up in faith says, "We can do this! This is not a problem. I am convinced that God will do it." Think of Peter after he has been filled with the Holy Spirit in Acts 2. He is no longer running to his past and saying "I'm going fishing." He is the first to stand up and preach the gospel of the resurrected Christ! He is also walking in such boldness and power that people are being healed in the streets just by getting within shadow's distance of him (Acts 5:15). This doesn't sound like the same guy that denied his relationship with Jesus three times in a few hours. When the sick are brought to him his faith is saying "we can do this!"

If you are going to partner with Holy Spirit to bring God's gifts to others—gifts of healing, wisdom, revelation and breakthrough—you will have to see things from God's perspective with a spirit of faith. And it's the Holy Spirit in you that will make that happen. Praying in the Spirit is one way that we release the Holy Spirit to work in our lives.

Another powerful benefit of spiritual language is that it makes us "God-inside minded"—aware of His presence and voice. We become more conscious of God's constant working

...spiritual language taps the believer into God's mind and heart for others. day by day and moment by moment. This "God-inside-mindedness" is more tuned in to the Spirit's voice. The veil between the spiritual and the natural gets thinner and thinner. We come to understand that God's reality is not dissected as the natural and spiritual, the temporal and eternal. To God it's all one reality. Spiritual language can become as common to a Spirit-filled believer as his natural speech, which certainly makes the operation of the Spirit something that is expected, not an oddity.

Certainly, a fourth benefit is that spiritual language taps the believer into God's mind and heart for others. What is the result of the indwelling Holy Spirit in the believer? Among numerous other benefits, *the Holy Spirit fills our heart with the love of God for others.* Paul tells the Romans, *"...the love of God has been poured out in our hearts by the Holy Spirit who was given to us"* (Romans 5:5). Every believer knows God pours His love into our hearts. We know that the Holy Spirit comes into a believer when he is born again. But the King James catches a nuance that is important in Romans 5:5 saying, "The love of God has been shed abroad in our hearts..." This is a picture of fullness and overflow which is the very nature of our infinite God. Consequently, Jesus' desire for us is that we would be so filled that rivers of life-giving water would pour out of our inner man so that we would be a blessing to many. This is what Jesus says, *"Out of your inner most being will flow rivers of living water"* (John 7:38), which John, in verse 39, directly associates with the Spirit-outpouring of Acts 2.

Whether we call it "stirring up the Holy Spirit", "releasing the Spirit" or "activating the Spirit" (these are all painfully limiting terminologies for the infinite God at work in us), we are referring to our willingness and ability to partner with what Holy Spirit wants to give us from God and give through us to others. This is also seen in how limited our understanding is in prayer. The Holy Spirit, who knows what and how we need to pray, helps us in our lack of knowledge. When we pray in the Spirit, releasing the

Spirit to pray through us in spiritual language, the infinite supply of His love for others gets activated in us. *"We don't know how to pray as we ought, but the Spirit himself makes intercession for us with groanings too deep for words... according to the will of God"* (Romans 8:26-27).[9]

Praying in the Spirit regularly is not weird. Paul charges the church at Ephesus, and all those churches that would read this travelling (circular) letter, to *"always pray in the Spirit... for all the saints"* (Ephesians 6:18). Employing our spiritual language regularly helps us get more comfortable with partnering with the Spirit, builds up our faith to see the way God sees, makes us "God-inside minded," taps us into God's loving heart for others and opens us to pray for others according to the will of God. To pray in the Spirit daily is a huge part of stirring up the gifts.

Let me explain this daily discipline in a practical way.

I received Spirit Baptism at the age of nine so when I was a teen I knew about praying in the Spirit. But I had never been told that praying in the Spirit was something I could do on a daily basis. I waited, like everyone else, for the one or two revival meetings each year when "the Spirit would fall" and we would be filled again. I didn't know that the Spirit had been poured out on the earth once and there was no need for Him to be poured out again (sometimes our Old Testament terminologies lock us into Old Testament expectations). Nor did anyone teach me that "the spirit of the prophet is subject to the prophet" or that the only way Paul could tell them to speak "one by one" in the Spirit is for the speaker to have control over the speaking (1 Corinthians 14:29, 32). No one told me what Paul meant when he said, *"What am I to do? I will pray with my spirit, but I will pray with my mind also; I will sing praise with my spirit, but I will sing with my mind also"* (14:15). But all of that changed when a missionary from Africa spoke in my church one week and explained the "discipline of spiritual language." On that day, I learned something that changed my life forever.

I learned that I didn't have to wait for the flaming evangelist to come to town, or for the once-a-year youth camp experience.

I learned that the Holy Spirit is always "on" and I'm the one that is "off" and "on." I learned that I can pray in the Spirit "at will." I learned that my prayer language is different from the manifestation gifts of the Spirit in that my prayer language is as I will ("*I will pray with my spirit...*" 1 Corinthians 14:15) and the manifestation gifts for the congregation are as the Spirit wills (1 Corinthians 12:11). The reality is, even our partnership in the operation of the gifts involves our will or else Paul could not say, "*Let all things be done, decently and in order*" (14:31). If we don't have the responsibility to put order into the operation of the gifts—if the Holy Spirit just takes over our body and makes us do something beyond our control, Paul's admonition would be meaningless. Praying in the Spirit daily actually prepares us for the occasions when the Holy Spirit wills to work through us. It's a partnership.

So I learned to pray in the Spirit on a daily basis—in the "in-betweens." I liken this practice to the thin sliver of mortar between the bricks in a wall. It seems like the minor part but it is what holds the wall together. Praying in the Spirit daily as a discipline is learning to pray in the in-betweens; between the bedroom and the kitchen, between the home and the office, between the office and the grocery store. I learned to fill the in-betweens of my days with prayer language—not boisterous or obnoxious prayer, but quietly audible prayer in the Spirit. I learned that this is the key to "living in the Spirit" and "minding the things of the Spirit" (Romans 8:4-5). I discovered that if I would pray in the Spirit for a few minutes before going to sleep at night, it would impact the thoughts I would wake up to the next morning. I discovered that I could invite Holy Spirit to train my thoughts in the night time. "*I will bless the Lord, who hath given me counsel: my reins also instruct me in the night seasons*" (Psalm 16:7).

I learned that by praying in the Spirit in the in-betweens I became much more attuned to the Spirit's voice to hear any instructions He would give about speaking or ministering to someone with a gift of the Spirit from the Father's heart.

My wife and I were flying to Great Britain to minister. I was sitting on an aisle seat and my wife was in the middle seat with an elderly lady on the window seat on the other side. One row ahead of me and across the aisle sat a young, strikingly attractive woman. Over a period of time I began to sense the Lord giving me a word for this woman, but I questioned within myself whether this was the Lord or my own sense of attraction. But the word became clearer and persistent. So I said to the Lord, "If that is really You, and not just my flesh, then give me a word for this grandma sitting on the other side of my wife." And he immediately did. He gave me a word of knowledge about this older woman's granddaughter who was far away from God and how concerned she was for her. I told my wife what was going on and the struggle I was feeling. She agreed that I should give this word to the older woman.

As I introduced myself to the woman on the window of my row, and began to share what I sensed about her granddaughter, she began to weep. Then she recounted some details of the story to my wife and me, and I knew this was not only God speaking to me about the older woman, but also about the young lady seated ahead. But now my wife knows what is going on and is in full agreement that I need to share this word with the young woman as well. But the plane is about to land. Timing is also something that we have a responsibility for in the distribution of the gifts.

I got the young woman's attention and simply said, "My wife and I feel like we need to speak with you. Can we talk to you in the concourse of the airport after we get off the plane?" She agreed. Once we disembarked and introduced ourselves, I proceeded to share that I saw her at the head of the long table in a board room; that God was promoting her and that she should not be afraid— that God wanted to use her and that He loved her. This gave us the opportunity to pray with her as well.

I have not seen or heard of that woman since, but I know she was blessed to know God had a good plan for her life and He loves her. I also know that I would not have been able to rightly discern the Holy Spirit's voice in that situation if I had not made a habit of praying in the Spirit daily and tuning my ear to hear.

Develop a Dynamic Devotional Life

The idea of a "dynamic devotional life" may sound strange, even intimidating to some. By dynamic, I simply mean an active, conversational exchange between two persons that have something to say to each other. By "dynamic devotions" I mean more than reading the Bible or a devotional guide five to fifteen minutes per day. **God wants a continual conversation with us just like He had with Adam and Eve,** walking with them "in the cool of the day" (morning and evening). A conversation is more than reading a letter from a friend (as good as that may be). A conversation includes asking questions and listening for the answers. It consists of talking about the good, the bad and the ugly of life and hearing from your friend, both His perspective, but especially His support and love for you in the midst of it.

Have you learned to read the Scriptures, then put yourself in the stories you're reading and turn them into conversation? For example, have you learned to say, "Father, I see here how Samson misunderstood Your faithful power in his life for permission to get lazy with his promises to You. In what ways do You see that happening in me?" Or, "Abba, I see how completely Jesus trusted You and only did what He saw You doing. Am I trusting You like that? Talk to me about how I can trust You more explicitly..." If our "devotions" are not real conversations with talking, asking, listening and knowing (learning about ourselves and the other), it's not going to be life-giving. No wonder we've turned it into another box to check off our religious list.

When God speaks to you His speaking is life-giving. Jesus said, "His commands (instructions, directions) are life" and His speaking is how He is working in you. *"The words that I speak to you are not just my own. Rather, it is the Father, living in Me, Who is doing His work"* (John 14:10). *"I know that His* **When God speaks to you His speaking is life-giving.** *command leads to eternal life. So whatever I say is just what the Father has told Me to say"* (John 12:50). Jesus is saying, "when I do what the Father speaks in me, it is life-giving and brings healing, wholeness and life to people, so I only speak what the Father speaks to Me." He is not talking about commands as "thou shalt nots," but what He hears the Father saying to Him in His times of prayer. He gets directions from the Father, prophetic words, words of wisdom, words of knowledge, discerning of spirits, gifts of healings... then He goes out and gives those away.

Many believers think Jesus did what He did, knew what He knew and said what He said because he was God. But Jesus willingly laid aside the ability to act unilaterally as God, and chose to partner with the Holy Spirit—to depend upon Holy Spirit to give to Him the things the Father wanted to say and do (see Acts 10:38). He did this, among other reasons, to demonstrate what the Son of Man was meant to do as partner with God. He did this so that you and I would see how we are to live in partnership with the Spirit of God so that *"these same works you will do because I go to my Father"* (John14:12).

Many believers struggle to spend time with God because they subconsciously believe it is only punching the clock on a requirement, proving their commitment to God, or staying "grounded" with a few Scriptures a day. Many believers go through the motions of "daily devotions;" but they don't really expect to hear from God. They don't even have a paper and pen/pencil (or laptop) with them because they don't expect to hear something worth writing down.

When I was younger I despised habit and routine. I would go out of my way to change things up, rearrange the furniture, wear different clothes, or drive a different way to work. This also applied to my devotions. In fact, I didn't have any regularity in my devotional life; I struggled fiercely and usually with shame and disappointment about how intermittent my times with God would be. I would do really well for a week or two and then slide back into old habits. As I have grown older I have become more comfortable with routine, seeing the benefits of a few important things that need to be done daily. What I have discovered about my time with the Lord is that it is a living, intimate time (most of the time), where I am not just reading a couple of passages

—boldness comes from time spent with God, and in those times, hearing His voice. from Scripture, but turning those passages into conversation with God, and listening. I bring worship music into my time with God and sing to Him, often finding tears flowing down my cheeks as I open my heart to Him, praying in the Spirit and calling out to Him for my family, friends, and needs around the world. It is in these times that I experience the intimacy Jesus shared when He referred to the Father as "Abba" (Daddy) and discover again and again what is on Abba's heart.

One thing I can say with certainty: boldness comes from time spent with God, and in those times, hearing His voice. When God speaks a word, brings a thought to life, talks to me about someone or something, and especially when He is talking to me about how much He loves me—I look at that day differently. I have a sense of purpose about that day. I have a boldness to speak to people, say things and do things I would not do if I had not had that time with God. You don't have to be super-spiritual or even to have daily devotions to stir up the gifts; but you will certainly walk in a more acute hunger for God, maintain a clearer sense of mission and a boldness in knowing that you are "carrying something" when you practice the presence of God daily.[10]

MEDITATE UPON THE WORD DAILY

Meditation is perceived in Western Christianity as the domain of Eastern religions (Hinduism, Buddhism, Taoism, etc.)—we tend to think yoga or transcendental meditation. In reality, meditation is a Christian practice (and, in fact, Christianity originated as an Eastern religion). The difference between Christian meditation and that of the other religions is as big as the difference between the spirit (*pneuma*) and the soul (*psuche*). **Christian meditation is a spirit-centered practice**, whereas Eastern cult meditation is a mental or soulish one. Those who are not born again in their spirits cannot meditate as Christians do, the Holy Spirit bringing God's Word to life in a person's spirit.

But equally important, meditating on the Word of God is not to be confused with Scripture reading, Scripture memory or some mental exercise. Meditation on Scripture involves intently considering the truth of Scripture, personalizing the Scripture and repeatedly speaking the words of Scripture (or whatever God is saying) to yourself. The Hebrew *hagah* literally means to chew on, to mutter, and to speak continually. So Moses' admonition to Joshua becomes clear, *"This Book of the Law shall not depart from your mouth, but you shall meditate in it day and night..."* (Joshua 1:8). Through meditation of Scripture the truth is moved eighteen inches from my heart to my head. That is, what we have known in our spirit (our "knower") by the Holy Spirit, but are largely unaware of with our mind (in our "thinker"), becomes conscious reality in our minds. Meditation on Scripture is the means by which you replace information with revelation— cognitive analog thinking with digital knowing, snail speed with warp speed.

My pastor used to say, "There are three types of people in church; the self-conscious, the God-conscious and the unconscious." Of course, everyone would laugh. Most of us at least start out as self-conscious. We are mostly aware of self and circumstances. We grow spiritually to discern God's presence and voice. The role of my will is to choose which "consciousness" I want to be governed by.

But just knowing the Scriptures is not enough either. Jesus told the Pharisees—the most ardent pursuers of scriptural knowledge in His day—*"You search the Scriptures for in them you think you have life, and these are they which testify of Me, but you are not willing to come to Me that you may have life"* (John 5:39-40). They knew the Scriptures, but didn't know Him, the Prince of Life. Through meditation I acknowledge the inadequacy of mere scriptural knowledge and the necessity of the illuminating work of the Holy Spirit. Through meditation I submit my mind, will, and emotions to God.

What happens when we meditate on the Word? In short, God's words are not just suggestions or information. His words are life—they uphold and sustain all creation (Hebrews 1:3), and they create reality in us. When God speaks "Peace" to you, He is not suggesting you should worry less, He is actually imparting peace into your spirit and soul! His words create. The Word of God, in the hands of the Holy Spirit is transformed in our spirit from the written Scriptures (*graphe*), to the Living Word (*logos*), to a personal transforming reality, a spoken word (*rhema*) to us that carries life. Listen to how the Scriptures describe this transformational action:

My heart was hot within me; while I was musing (meditating), the fire burned. Then I spoke with my tongue. (Psalm 39:3).

But His word was in my heart like a burning fire shut up in my bones; I was weary of holding it back, and I could not (Jeremiah 20:9).

Did not our heart burn within us while He talked with us on the road, and while He opened the Scriptures to us? (Luke 24:32).

Fire effects a transformational process that converts a material solid into a liquid or a gas. Fire will consume a log of wood (a solid) and transform it into flames and smoke (a gas). It will melt ice (a solid) into water (a liquid) and then to vapor (gas). The work of the Holy Spirit is a "baptism of fire"—the transformational process. His words grow hot within us, a fire burns. It comes alive in us, and actually becomes our life. When we meditate upon the Word of God something happens inside our spirit. Our hard heart gets pliable again. We yield our will. We grow and change on the inside. Smith Wigglesworth said, "I am a thousand times bigger on the inside than I am on the outside." What does that mean? When we gaze on the face of

Jesus we are transformed from glory to glory (2 Corinthians 3:18). This is the work of the Spirit in us.

...there are two primary exercises of the spirit man (*pneuma*); praying in the spirit and meditating the Word of God.

Over the course of a few decades of pastoral ministry I have come to the conclusion that there are two primary exercises of the spirit man (pneuma); praying in the spirit and meditating the Word of God. Both are a dynamic partnership between the human spirit and the indwelling Holy Spirit. Those who desire spiritual growth and yet fail to meditate upon the Scriptures only limit the tools the Holy Spirit has available to minister through them to others. Those who do not meditate on Scripture will stall in their spiritual growth or mistake head knowledge for spiritual maturity. There is no lightning bolt of anointing that will fix this shortage of internal transformation that comes through the combination of meditation on the Word and spiritual language.

Here's What I've Learned

For some reason we hear very little said, and even less modeled, regarding the meditation of the Word. Can I, as a learner, share with you something I've learned?

I meditate especially the words of Jesus as found in the Gospels and Jesus' revelation through the Apostle Paul. I spend time almost daily (with occasional misses, for sure) in worship, prayer and reading the Scriptures. Most of the time, I go to bed at night anticipating my time with the Lord the next morning—I know He wants to talk with me. It hasn't always been this way! Earlier in my life I struggled to discipline myself to be with God. But crises happen, tragedies come, friendships ebb and priorities change.

While I am reading the Scriptures there is usually a verse or a passage of Scripture that comes alive to me. We say, "It leaps off the page." When that happens, I write that verse or passage down, usually on a large 4 inch by 6 inch "Post-it" note. I spend 10 or 15 minutes at least, just reading over, pondering, and saying that verse again and again. I ask the Lord what He wants to say to me about that. I personalize the verse—re-word it into the First person singular—so it is talking about me. In other words, I put myself into the Scripture. The same way Jesus *"found the place where it was written of Him..."* (Luke 4:17-18), I find myself in the Scripture. When Paul says, *"I have been crucified with Christ and it's no longer I that live but Christ that lives in me..."* (Galatians 2:20), I declare the same about me. If it's true about Paul because he is in Christ, then it's also true about me because I am also in Christ.

After I have written that verse out by hand on the post-it note and spend some time pondering it, muttering it, personalizing it, then I put it in the cover of my Bible with the other verses I am meditating on. I carry a dozen or so verses in my Bible cover all the time, and pull them out a few times over the course of a few days to meditate.

Here are the verses that are in my Bible cover right now:

Most assuredly, I say to you, the hour is coming, and now is, when the dead will hear the voice of the Son of God; and those who hear will live (John 5:25).

As the living Father sent Me, and I live because of the Father, so he who feeds on Me will live because of Me (John 6:57).

Jesus answered them and said, "My doctrine is not Mine, but His who sent Me" (John 7:16).

Jesus answered and said to them, "Even if I bear witness of Myself, My witness is true, for I know where I came from and where I am going; but you do not know where I come from and where I am going" (John. 8:14).

And He said to them, "You are from beneath; I am from above. You are of this world; I am not of this world" (John 8:23).

For I have not spoken on My own authority; but the Father who sent Me gave Me a command, what I should say and what I should speak. And I know that His command is everlasting life. Therefore, whatever I speak, just as the Father has told Me, so I speak (John. 12:49-50).

Do you not believe that I am in the Father, and the Father in Me? The words that I speak to you I do not speak on My own authority; but the Father who dwells in Me does the works (John. 14:10).

[Paul spent his last days] preaching the kingdom of God and teaching the things which concern the Lord Jesus Christ with all confidence, no one forbidding him. (Acts 28:31).

I thank my God always concerning you for the grace of God which was given to you by Christ Jesus, that you were enriched in everything by Him in all utterance and all knowledge, even as the testimony of Christ was confirmed in you, so that you come short in no gift, eagerly waiting for the revelation of our Lord Jesus Christ (1 Corinthians 1:4-7).

Blessed be the God and Father of our Lord Jesus Christ, who has blessed us with every spiritual blessing in the heavenly places in Christ (Ephesians 1:3).

...till we all come to the unity of the faith and of the knowledge of the Son of God, to a perfect man, to the measure of the stature of the fullness of Christ (Ephesians 4:13).

These verses may not seem like good "meditation ground" to you, but as a teacher of the Word, I can assure you that I spend a lot of time meditating on a spirit of wisdom and revelation, authority to preach the kingdom of God, and to know what my Father is saying, and to say only that. I spend a lot of time meditating on my identification with Christ in his death, burial and resurrection, and on my position around the heavenly throne before the Father. I see myself continually coming boldly before the Father in Jesus the High Priest.

Scripture itself tells us what to meditate upon:

- The Person and being of God:

When I remember You on my bed, I meditate on You in the night watches (Psalm 63:6).

I will meditate on the glorious splendor of Your majesty... (Psalm 145:5).

- His words, statutes and precepts:

Blessed is the man . . . [whose] delight is in the law of the Lord, and in His law he meditates day and night (Psalm 1:1-2; cf. 119:15, 23, 47, 148).

- His ways and works:

I will also meditate on all Your work, and talk of Your deeds (Psalm 77:12).

So shall I meditate on Your wonderful works (Psalm 119:47).

- His Name:

So a book of remembrance was written before Him for those who fear the Lord and who meditate on His name (Malachi 3:16).

- My Identification with Christ

Meditate upon these things; give yourself entirely to them; that your progress may appear to all (1 Timothy 4:15).

I suppose I don't have to connect the dots for you as to why this is critical for those who wish to be in active partnership with Holy Spirit. What we meditate upon is what is alive in us. If we don't meditate upon the Word there is nothing alive in us. The simple principle is this: *a breakthrough in revelation will precede every other breakthrough in one's life*. And revelation is first a spiritual reality before it is a mental one. We can gather sermon notes and load up on downloaded information, but there is no life or power in it. Songwriters can insert the cliché worship phrases, but it doesn't give life to the congregation that sings it. But when we meditate on the Word, it will burn like a fire on the inside, and then we will speak (or write). The prophetic will be constantly activated in us. The arsenal with which the Holy Spirit will have access to speak from our spirit will be multi-faceted; like choosing from a variety of weapons in an armory. Meditate in the Word day and night. Get your gun loaded, your quiver full, so that the Holy Spirit has multiple resources to draw out of your spirit and understanding.

PRACTICE INTENTIONAL COMPASSION

Many have a strong desire to be used of God but simply don't know where to start. If you a few friends, acquaintances, or relatives, you have a starting place. Start with your children, your

If you want to be used of God, simply be intentionally compassionate. parents or siblings. Write down two or three people's names in the morning and pray over them, asking Holy Spirit to give you a word in due season for them. **"Lord, what would You like to say to them that would bless them and let them know You are thinking about them?"** Write down what you sense God is saying—prophetic words or verses—to give to someone. If you have been meditating in the Scriptures, these words will be alive in you. When you speak out what is alive in you, it produces life in those who hear it. Pray also for those in leadership over you; ask God to use you to bless them.

A couple of years ago Chiqui and I attended our church's New Year's Eve service. We had been invited to a couple of New Year's parties but at the conclusion of the service we felt we were to go home and celebrate quietly together. When we arrived home we felt stirred to pray. (As I reflect on my life I found many of my New Year's Eves have been in prayer—giving thanks for what the Lord has done the previous year and asking for Him to speak about the year ahead.) So Chiqui and I sat on the floor of our living room and began to pray. We made a list of ten couples that are significant to us; either leaders over us or couples we serve in leadership. We both began to pray over each couple separately, and immediately the Holy Spirit began to give us prophetic words for these couples, and we were both writing what we were hearing. After an hour or so, we felt an end to this stirring, and began to compare notes. These words were an amazing confirmation to both of us that the Lord wanted to bless these friends. On New Year's Day I spent the morning combining Chiqui's prophetic thoughts about each couple with my own, and emailing those to proper recipients. We received such warm responses from each couple, encouraged with God's plans and thoughts for them for the New Year. Do you think that was a powerful way to start our new year? Absolutely.

If you want to be used of God, simply be intentionally compassionate. Choose to wait on God for someone else. Write down what you hear for someone else. Decide that you are going to pray for someone when you go to church this weekend. Decide to speak a word of blessing and confirmation to someone at work today. Sit down and write a letter or email to someone you know has been through some rough waters. Ask the Lord to give you a picture, a word, a verse of Scripture that would be a blessing to them. You don't have to say, "Thus saith the Lord," or even "God gave me this for you..." Just bless them and watch what God does. Remember to always minister words of edification, exhortation and comfort; words that lift and encourage.

I have made a practice over the years of mentoring young men. That's part of my intentional compassion. As I am deliberate to schedule times to sit with these guys I find I am in an other-centered position to give away something that I have. I often find myself driving to these coffees or breakfasts asking the Lord to flow through me with a word of knowledge, a word of wisdom or a prophetic word or prophetic question. Tonight, for example, just before sitting down to write this section, I was meeting with a young man who feels stuck. He is between ministry assignments, his wife is tired of her job and anxious. He described her "sense of heaviness" and how they are feeling the need to "bare down and do some fasting of TV and other possible distractions." It all sounded good, even right, but as he was speaking I heard that inner voice say, "If you don't balance the fast with a spirit of generosity you will become more and more introspective and depressed." Then I heard, "Is not this the fast that I have chosen..." I instantly knew it was from Isaiah 58:

Is this not the fast that I have chosen...
Is it not to share your bread with the hungry,
And that you bring to your house the poor who are cast out;
When you see the naked, that you cover him,
And not hide yourself from your own flesh?
Then your light shall break forth like the morning,
Your healing shall spring forth speedily,
And your righteousness shall go before you. (Isaiah 58:6-8)

I knew the Lord was giving me a prophetic word, a *rhema* word for this couple. The enemy loves to play on our fears and make us so self-conscious that we actually close in on ourselves and hold things close. It is the opposite of what we need to be—intentionally compassionate. There is something about giving to others that opens the floodgates of God's provision and gets us unstuck. As I shared what I was sensing, this young man knew the Lord had put His finger on a key for them. He was excited and couldn't wait to get home to share the word with his wife. But who left that mentoring session feeling more energized, more nourished—the young man who received the word or the guy that gave the word? I'm sure I did. Being intentionally compassionate always puts us in a place to be used of God.

Discussion Questions

1. Why does the author assert that spiritual language as a daily discipline is the best way to get comfortable partnering with the Holy Spirit?

2. How do you cultivate a daily awareness of Holy Spirit's presence?

3. What are some ways our devotional times with the Lord can become a catalyst for the operation of the gifts to bless others?

Chapter Twelve

Ways to Cultivate the Gifts, Part 2

Practice the Laying on of Hands

The laying on of hands is not only a doctrine of the Church (Heb. 6:2), it is a doctrine because it is a spiritual principle through which God works in people. Jesus said that hands are to be laid on the sick and they will recover (Mark 16:17-18), hands are laid on people for gifts to be imparted (1 Timothy 4:14), and for ordination of ministry (1 Timothy 5:22). These can become mechanical actions unless we understand that God is a relational, connecting God. He gives gifts out of His overflowing Spirit through others because He wants us to be connected and to live out a relational kingdom. **It should not be surprising to us that many facets of ministry happen through the touch.** It represents the incarnation of God into the world He has made.

What I have found by practical experience, which I cannot totally explain, is that quite often the gifts of the Spirit do not begin to flow in me toward a person until I lay my hands on them to minister. There are times the Lord gives me a gift of a word of knowledge, a gift of a word of wisdom or prophecy for someone before I see them. As a pastor for several decades, there a number of times the Lord has given me "a word" for someone during the week or before I arrived at a service or a meeting. But more often it is when I lay hands on people that He begins to speak things in my spirit for them.

If you desire the gifts of the Spirit to be released in your life, know that there may be times that a physical touch (when and where appropriate) may release gifts of the Spirit through you. Yes, precautions have to be taken anytime we are ministering to others, especially people of the other gender. Some have been physically or sexually abused and are not comfortable with someone they don't know connecting in any way physically. Sometimes we can touch people in inappropriate ways (either for us or them) that is distracting. But Jesus touched people that shouldn't be touched according to cultural norms, and we shouldn't let the enemy paralyze us from ministering to people if we take godly precautions to honor the dignity and sensitivities of the people to whom we minister. So here a few common sense guidelines to consider:

- First, ask the person's name (if it's not known); there is dignity in knowing one another. Personal ministry is not a mechanical assembly line of dispensing God, it is a personal connection of one believer to another in the blessing of the Triune God.

- Ask the person if you may lay a hand on their shoulder to pray. If they are hesitant, don't.

- Don't lay hands on a person's head unless you stand in a place of confirmed authority (as pastor, ordaining elder, etc.) over them. There is something about the "head" that represents authority in the things of the Spirit; I am very careful about who I allow to lay hands on my head. Evidently both good and bad can be imparted through the laying of hands (1 Timothy 5:22), and we should know well those who would lay hands on our heads.

- Keep your eyes open when laying hands on someone so you can see what physical reactions or facial expressions might inform you as to receptivity and response to what God is doing.

- When ministering healing, don't ask God to do something; speak to the physical condition, the organ, the system, the body. We have the authority in Jesus' Name (Mark 16:17-18). We command sickness to leave and healing to flow. Most believers try to minister healing by talking to God rather than talking to the disease or infirmity. We take authority over that "name" (whatever the sickness or infirmity is) or that condition; in Jesus' name, commanding it to leave.

- Don't rub or stroke a person with your hand. This is probably more distracting than comforting unless you know the person well and they are of the same gender.

- Lead the person to hearing God's voice for themselves. "Father, what else do you want to say to_____ about what you are thinking about them?" And then be quiet long enough to let the Father speak to them.

These are the minimum suggestions. We should always be in touch with our motives for why we want to minister to a person. Keeping our heart humble and clear before God is each person's responsibility, no matter how long we have been ministering to others. Physical touch is a way in which wrong motives can be acted on most readily. We should be watchful, but bold.

In the ministry of all the gifts, I am not seeking to "have all the answers" or to be the local shaman where people can come for an "on-demand" healing or a word. I simply want to stay full of God and give Him away, as the Spirit directs, wherever there is need. But it is as the Spirit wills, not as I will. All of that being said, and with all of the precautions in view, God has empowered you to be a blessing to others, to make God famous for His unconditional goodness. You need to be more focused in your faith that God will get it right than the fear that you will do something wrong. Then you can boldly release God's compassion to others.

Spend Time with People that Move in the Gifts

This is probably the most common-sense point of them all, but if a person has not been around the things of the Spirit, that can be a great hurdle. **In any field of learning it is understood that best practices require a mentoring process.** That process starts with an "expert" modeling for a novice how something should be done well. The second stage is to do the task together (the mentor giving correction and instruction throughout the process), and the third stage is the expert/mentor allowing the protégé to do the task, watching, encouraging and advising as the learner joins knowledge with skill. But for some reason we mistakenly think this process can be skipped in spiritual things.

The fastest way to gain confidence in the operation of the gifts of the Spirit is to be around others that have experience partnering with Holy Spirit, ministering the gifts of the Spirit unselfishly and without fanfare. And you may ask, "But what if I don't know anybody that flows in the gifts like this?" If you don't know anyone with experience in the gifts, ask the Lord to connect you with someone. That connection can happen in numerous ways. It can mean attending a church (either regularly or for special instruction) that equips along these lines. It may be as simple as listening to teachings or reading books by those who have experience and are approved by a multitude of confirming voices.

If you have not been raised around the things of the Spirit

The fastest way to gain confidence in the operation of the gifts of the Spirit is to be around others that have experience partnering with Holy Spirit...

then you will have to venture outside of your normal channels of relationship. You may need to read books or listen to ministry by some that are new to you. Some churches, some denominations, even some nations and generations have moved in the gifts more than others. Read books by Smith Wigglesworth, John G. Lake, Lester Sumrall, Kenneth

Hagin, Aimee Semple McPherson, Jack Hayford, Bill Johnson, John Wimber, Oral Roberts, Reinhard Bonnke, etc. Read the Book of Acts and the Gospels repeatedly and ask the Lord to lead you to those who are walking out the ministry of Jesus in a Spirit-centered, biblical way.

The bottom line is that you need to "hang out" (in person, by books, CDs, MP3s, etc.) with people who see the operation of the gifts as "normal" before you will also see them as normal and live in the normative operation of the gifts of the Spirit.

PRACTICE IMMEDIATE OBEDIENCE

Our mind will always try to talk us out of obeying God. But **the more we obey, the stronger the Spirit's voice** (actually our hearing just gets trained better, more perceptive). The greatest enemy of immediate obedience is our analytical mind. Too often we won't receive a word from God unless we can understand it—we insist that God speak at the level of our minds:

Think about the occasion when Gabriel comes to Mary to announce the incredible news of the Christ-child, Gabriel says:

"The Holy Spirit will come upon you, and the power of the Highest will overshadow you; therefore, also, that Holy One who is to be born will be called the Son of God. Now indeed, Elizabeth your relative has also conceived a son in her old age; and this is now the sixth month for her who was called barren. For with God nothing will be impossible" (Luke 1:35-37).

In essence, Gabriel is saying, "No word of God is void of power—it has in it the power to fulfill what it declares..."

A spirit of immediate obedience says, "God, even if I don't understand it, speak it to me anyway and I will obey." We look around and ask, "Who's the smartest guy in the room? Let's follow him and do what he says." But God is asking, "Who in this room is not afraid of looking foolish? Who is willing to do whatever I tell him?"

The Lord tells Joshua to have the people of Israel, not known for their ability to control their tongues, to quietly march around the walls of Jericho seven days and then seven times on the last day. The angel of the Lord tells Gideon to trim the army down to 300 and light lanterns, break pitchers and blow horns. The prophet tells a high-ranking Syrian officer to go dip seven times in a muddy river for healing of leprosy. One prophet tells the impoverished woman to go borrow all the jars and pitchers she can find, and another asks a widow to bake him a stack of pancakes first, using the last bit of Aunt Jemima's pancake mix that she possesses. Jesus tells Peter to go catch a fish and pull the coin out of its mouth to pay the taxes. God's ways don't make sense to the natural mind.

It was the Holy Spirit that told Jesus to put spit on the mute's tongue for his speech to be restored. And it was the Holy Spirit that told Jesus to spit on the ground and make a mud pack to smear on a blind man's eyes. It was the Holy Spirit that told Jesus to stop the funeral procession already in progress and command the dead boy to come to life. It was the Holy Spirit that told Jesus to lay His hand on the leper's contagious head. We don't think that took any faith for Jesus, but of course it did. Jesus did His mighty works the same way you and I do; by the obedience of faith. Jesus also learned immediate obedience. This is part of the things he learned through suffering. There is a suffering, a mental anguish that is involved in faith. There is a laying of my analytical mind on the altar of sacrifice in order to obey God.

A lot believers want God to work, but then when He asks us to do something we say, "Well, if it's not stupid I'll do it..." And the Lord will say, "No, it's really stupid! It will look totally crazy to your natural mind!" Our analytical, culturally-compressed mind is screaming, "This is crazy! What will people think!? What if it doesn't work?" Take the risk. Obey what you hear God saying.

Pastors and Bible college deans hate to see this kind of encouragement to take action because we know that some young eager believer will "try it." When I was in Bible College I heard a story that happened on that campus decades earlier of a student that didn't have any money, but he was almost in violation of the hair code (that will give you a hint of how long ago this happened). He didn't know what to do so he prayed. He felt God told him to go to the barber shop, without money, and it would be OK. The young Bible college student was learning to walk by faith, so he went. He waited his turn for the barber chair, and all the while, had a war going on in his mind. "What happens if I get the haircut and then have to tell the barber I don't have the money?" "What if... what if... what if..." His turn came and he somewhat sheepishly took his seat in the barber chair. While he was getting his haircut someone he didn't know came into the barber shop and put the money in his hand.

Years later, the same young man had become a successful preacher/teacher and was back at the same Bible College, his alma mater, to speak. The Dean asked him not to share that story with the student body. When the student-now-speaker asked why not, the Dean said, "Because we have a lot of young idealistic students here that will go out and try something foolish." So he told it again.

We pastors temper what we say because we know someone will try it, and they may fail, and it may make someone look bad, and pastors may have to go "clean up a mess" or "put out a fire." But I would rather spend my days cleaning up some "faith messes" than to have a church full of analytical minds that will never obey the voice of the Spirit and subsequently, never see God do mighty things!

There are two types of failure. One is the failure due to inexperience; the other is the failure due to disobedience and rebellion. The prophet Samuel told Saul to kill all the enemy, to leave no one alive. But Saul didn't obey. When Samuel called him to account Saul blamed the people, "the people wanted to spare the spoil for themselves... I wanted to offer this as sacrifice." This lack of fear of God cost Saul his throne (1 Samuel 15:10-15).

The prophet told the king to strike the arrows on the ground before he died. The king struck the ground three times. But the prophet was angry that he only struck the ground three times... because the number of times he smote the ground determined the number of times God would smite the enemy. *"If you would have smote the ground six times the Lord would have smote the enemy until he was destroyed completely"* (2 Kings 13:15-19).

Sometimes immediate obedience is critical because it will save you from falling into a trap of unbelief, a disobedient spirit or even rebellion. Sometimes it is critical because the Lord has chosen to measure your victory by the same measure with which you obey.

A final thought on immediate obedience regarding things that seem strange to the natural mind. Leonard Sweet says:

Chaos is a better strategy for survival than order. It is not just that order can be reached out of chaos, or that one can only perceive chaos in relation to some perceived order. The emerging science of complexity, the generating science of post modernity, argues that chaos is essential to the emergence of order. Chaos and order coexist and emerge from one another.[11]

What does this mean? Even from a scientific perspective (for those who insist on some sense of analytical process), what your mind calls order may not be order at all, and what God calls order, may look like chaos to the natural mind. Just think about the upper room experience described in Acts 2. Jesus' grand culmination of ministry, crucifixion, mind-blowing resurrection and ascension out of the disciples' sight was not capped with a scene from Braveheart—with William Wallace astride his horse in front of the Scottish ragamuffin army, giving his troops a grand pep-talk to run into battle. On the contrary, Jesus tells them to go into Jerusalem and wait. Just wait. Then when they have waited for ten days, a strange sound fills the room, tongues of fire settle over each of their heads and they begin to speak in languages they have never learned. Chaos and order coexist and emerge from one another—but only God gets to determine which comes first.

The Church was not born in a committee meeting with strategies for the safest, most sensible approach to take the Gospel to the world. Nor do we have any record that lawyers were consulted regarding what should and shouldn't be said so as not to offend the cultural status quo. God's form of order looks like something that doesn't always look like order to us. Immediate obedience is something we can learn and grow in. And the one who obeys quickly will be much more likely to be partnering with Holy Spirit in the gifts He gives to those in need. And we may have to get to heaven before we know the ultimate impacts of our obedience. Don't judge too early.

He starts with us where we are and asks us to take small risks.

TAKE SMALL RISKS

It has been said that **the life of faith cannot afford the luxury of "risk-free living."** The previous idea of immediate obedience opens the idea of steps of faith and taking risk. The necessary dimension in learning to partner with Holy Spirit is to understand that He starts with you where you are and develops you in a process of training.

We want to jump to signs, wonders and miracles first. But the very desire probable means we aren't ready. Our priority is to be used of Him, to bless others, to minister wholeness where there is brokenness and peace where there is confusion and darkness. The motives are important, and the Holy Spirit knows how to bring us from point 'A' to point 'B' to point 'C' with maximum benefit to the Kingdom and minimal collateral damage. He starts with us where we are and asks us to take small risks.

The Bible college student that was stepping into the barber chair with no money (story from the previous point) was actually taking a small risk, though it would seem huge in the moment. His risk was $2 and some embarrassment. But it was a good first step that began to build a track record of faith in God.

Some might argue with me, but if you look at Jesus' ministry, there was minimal risk in his first miracle. He is turning water into wine among a crowd of people that had already had too much to drink. That's not to say Jesus was "trying out" his miracle powers to see if it would work. But clearly, He wasn't certain that this occasion was the starting place of His miracle ministry. He frankly told His mother, *"My time has not yet come."* But He called the servants to gather big pitchers of water; then out of the huge pitchers they drew wine—the best for last. Perhaps Jesus wanted something less conspicuous; perhaps it didn't matter.

Think about the first miracles the disciples of Jesus performed. Jesus told the disciples to set the hungry multitude in groups of fifty. Easy to do; not a big supernatural deal. Count to fifty, sit them down. Count to fifty, sit them down. Then Jesus lifted up a little bread and fish and blessed it. Then he handed it to them and told them to pass it out. It still doesn't seem like a big deal; it's something anyone could have done. But in the doing of what seemed natural, something supernatural happened. The more they distributed, the more was in their hands. I have a hunch that the first few pieces they broke off to give away were fairly small fragments. But then as they realized what was happening, they became more generous and broke larger and larger pieces off for the people. We know it was so because they ate until they were full and had twelve baskets left over on one occasion. (I just hope they made it back around to the first row of folks, apologized for their lack of faith and gave them seconds!) This is true for all of us. We start with small risks of faith, and grow into the greater challenges.

Perhaps this is why the gifts of "variety of tongues" (as a message to the assembly) and "interpretation of tongues" is one of the best places to start partnering with Holy Spirit. First of all, Spirit-filled believers are already praying in the Spirit. Speaking out a "message in tongues" in a group of worshippers is not much different than just speaking in tongues, except that it requires some partnership with another believer that will interpret. But the risk is very low. If no one interprets, nothing has been harmed in the gathering with the exception of a little embarrassment. But even then, who is it that should be embarrassed—the person who spoke out a message in another language or the person who should have interpreted but didn't? No one would really know. But it seems the primary benefit of a gifts of "diversity of tongues and interpretation" over a straightforward prophetic word, is that it is a low-risk way to begin to move in the gifts of the Spirit. The smaller the group, the smaller the risk.

Expect the Holy Spirit to give you some small steps to take in partnership with Him, then those invitations to supernatural partnership will get larger and larger.

LIVE WITH KINGDOM — INTENTIONALITY

Before concluding this section I want to re-visit and underscore the importance of intentionality. **We will never get started in partnering with Holy Spirit, in giving away His gifts, without being intentional toward Kingdom purposes.** Not only do we need to ask the Holy Spirit every day to use us—not only do we want to have conversations with the Lord regularly about what He wants us to do in His name today—we need to think through some strategies for Kingdom-intentionality. I am not suggesting that we set goals and strive to achieve them as a measurement of our "spiritual success." Being used of God to heal ten people versus three doesn't make us more spiritual. What I am suggesting is that we live with an awareness that God wants to shower the world with His compassion, and is inviting us to partner with Him in doing it. The issue is not how we do it, but that we look for opportunities to be a conduit of God's blessing.

I had lunch with a friend one day, and saw him do something with Kingdom-intentionality that changed me forever. The waitress approached our table, introduced herself and handed us the menus. She said politely, "I will be back in a few minutes after you've had time to look over the menu and decide what you want." But just before she left my friend spoke up and said, "Thank you,_____. And by the way, when you bring our food, we're going to be praying over our food. And since we are going to be praying, is there something you would like for us to pray about for you or your family? You can be thinking about that while we're making up our minds on our order." When the waitress came back, she took our order, and then my friend said, "Now what is it that we can pray for you?" I don't even remember what her request was, but I do remember she had thought about one. And I have done the same thing many times since that day. Every time, there is something—sometimes it is final exams coming up, sometimes it is a brother that's in trouble, sometimes it is their own need. And it always gives us an opportunity to bless someone else.

There are numerous other ways to be intentional in opening doors to give gifts. Write out words during your time with the Lord and take them with you; "Lord show me who this is for and how you want me to give it to them." Take a verse of Scripture that speaks blessing, peace, comfort or the Lord's love for us; simply say to someone, "Do you want to hear something I think will help you today?" and without waiting for an answer, just read the Scripture and follow it with a personal word of blessing.

My pastor, Robert Morris, tells of developing a practice of keeping a $50 bill in his wallet for a timely tip. With this spirit of generosity, he leaves this incredible tip for a waiter or waitress as the Lord prompts him. This is usually in a restaurant where he is intentional about dining regularly, so there is often an occasion for a follow-up conversation. The generosity alone provides a great open door to talk about the loving, overflowing nature of God (or just let the generosity speak for itself).

Whether it is a generous tip or an inquiry about family, ask them if there is something you can pray with them about. "I believe in prayer. I believe God loves you very much. And I believe He will hear us when we pray. Is there anything we can pray about for you?" That is a relatively non-threatening way to bless people because you are doing all the work and all the praying. Like Jesus, asking for what the disciples have to feed the multitude, taking it, holding it up to the Father and blessing it, then handing it to the disciples to do the easy part.

Don't you believe this world will be different if believers are daily, actively and intentionally looking for ways to make the Kingdom accessible to people? I know you do, and I know the Lord is giving ideas to you even now.

Discussion Questions

1. Which of the "cultivations" seems most important to you and why?

2. Which of the list do you hear the least about, and why do think this is so?

3. Which one of these would be the simplest for you to begin to cultivate into your own life?

4. What has the Lord said to you through the study of this chapter?

PART IV - FINAL THOUGHTS

CHAPTER THIRTEEN

THE PRIORITY IS THE PRESENCE

I initiated the previous section's "ten ways to cultivate the gifts" with Paul's exhortation to "covet, earnestly desire and ardently seek the gifts of the Spirit." But it's important to not let the dust settle on those thoughts without making it clear that the way we covet or earnestly seek the gifts is to seek the presence of the Gift-giver, not just the gift. Jesus didn't promise that the Father would send gifts; but He did promise that the Father would send a Person—the Holy Spirit—and with Him, we receive gifts. When the Church understands that the gifts of the Spirit are unending rivers of the Father, Son and Spirit's overflowing nature of infinite love, then seeking the gifts as a commodity is seen for what it is—the faulty notion of non-relational spiritual mechanics. God gives gifts because He is complete, has need of nothing, and overflows out of His infinite fullness. The key to partnering with the Holy Spirit in gift-giving is to be full of Him—filled with all the fullness of God (Ephesians 3:19). If a believer doesn't live in fullness, he will take all of God's gifts as a means to fill something of his own lack. He will tend to use the gifts upon himself (to make a name for himself or boost his ego). But true fullness comes in the

> **Jesus didn't promise that the Father would send gifts; but He did promise that the Father would send a Person—the Holy Spirit—and with Him, we receive gifts.**

passionate pursuit, not of the gifts, but of God himself.

This notion is so significant that it requires elaboration. Let's look at three biblical examples: Samuel, the archangel Gabriel, and that Apostle John.

SAMUEL WITH HIS WHOLE LIFE

When we think about the necessity of cultivating a life there is no story that more clearly speaks of submitting one's entirety to the presence of God than that of a boy named Samuel. He was dedicated from birth by a mother who was in her own right, an ardent seeker of a gift from the Lord. Hannah had been driven to seek the Lord for deliverance from a culturally induced harassment of barrenness. Once the Lord had granted her petition she was faithful to keep her vow to dedicate the child to the Lord's service.

Don't miss the contrast the Scripture portrays in the opening of young Samuel's story. The spiritual leadership of the day is lethargic and corrupt. Eli, the priest, is inattentive to the priority of instilling the fear of the Lord in his own sons. The sons, not surprisingly, have grown up despising the ways of the Lord; *"They were wicked men having no regard for the Lord"* (1 Samuel 2:12). Ultimately their abuse of the tithe caused the people to sin in that they became disillusioned with bringing the tithe to the Lord at all. We could say these were bad times for "the church" (to use the term 'church' for Old Testament Israel is to use it loosely). But the reading of this story in the Scripture portrays a sense that "on the outside" everything was corrupt, but inside the Temple Samuel was ministering to the Lord—*"meanwhile the boy Samuel grew up in the presence of the Lord"* (1 Samuel 2:21).

Perhaps you have not been raised around the presence of the Lord. Perhaps you have been exposed to corruption in leadership which caused you to lose hope "in the system." Perhaps, like the people of Israel at the time, you have given up on the prescribed way of the Lord because of abuses or inattentiveness. Samuel's story tells us that though this may be going on all around you, there is a secret place. There is a way to minister to the Lord, to grow up in the presence of the Lord when the world around you is consumed with other priorities. When the "older brothers" are working the system, and seemingly getting what they want, there is a place in the presence of the Lord that eventually makes all the difference. Our hindsight allows us to see that long after these corrupt sons of Eli are dead, Samuel was anointing kings and bringing salvation to Israel. He learned in his youth how to "stay full" in a land of spiritual famine, and the day came when, his own fullness ushered a flow prophetic accuracy, a disbursement of gifts and anointings that literally guided God's people into the next era of promise.

Samuel's story does not dictate that we have to get started with God when we are children or else it is too late. The lives of the Apostle Paul, Moses, Abraham and the thief hanging beside Jesus on the cross, all attest that such is not the case. To the contrary, Samuel's story teaches that no matter how we were raised or what environment surrounds us, we can find that place in the presence of God that makes the difference. We can learn to cultivate the habit of praise, the environment of worship—especially with all the technological means we have at our disposal to select our own environment and pump it in through earbuds. We can choose the presence of God, God's praises, God's people, and find that fullness is the key to overflow, and overflow is how we partner with Holy Spirit in dispensing God's gifts to those in need

The priority, no matter what era we may be living in, is the presence of God. The way to partner with God's agenda is a personal ongoing fullness in the Holy Spirit that comes in the presence of the Lord.

Gabriel's Identity is Not Might and Power

Let us consider the experiences Daniel had with an archangel so overwhelming and awe-inspiring that Daniel fell on his face as one dead in his presence. When he describes this incredible being from another world he says:

I lifted my eyes and looked, and behold, a certain man clothed in linen, whose waist was girded with gold of Uphaz! His body was like beryl, his face like the appearance of lightning, his eyes like torches of fire, his arms and feet like burnished bronze in color, and the sound of his words like the voice of a multitude (Daniel 10:5-6).

His appearance was powerful and overwhelming.

Though Gabriel never identifies himself by name in this passage, scholars make an educated assumption of this archangel's identity because he says the only one helping him in the cosmic battle against the prince of Persia is the archangel Michael (Daniel 10:13), and after delivering the message to Daniel, he must return to the battle because the angelic Prince of Greece is joining the battle (Daniel 10:20). With such a glorious appearance one might think it odd that this archangel does not readily identify himself by name. But there is no quest for branding here. In fact, both Gabriel and Michael have seen firsthand what happens from such a self-promoting venture. Lucifer, another archangel was cast out of heaven for such pandering. So Gabriel's humility should not surprise us. The next time we see Gabriel, he does identify himself, in a way in which we should take note.

Zachariah, the father-to-be of John the Baptist, is on his priestly rotation at the Temple:

According to the custom of the priesthood, his lot fell to burn incense when he went into the temple of the Lord.

And the whole multitude of the people was praying outside at the hour of incense. Then an angel of the Lord appeared to him, standing on the right side of the altar of incense. And when Zacharias saw him, he was troubled, and fear fell upon him. But the angel said to him, "Do not be afraid, Zacharias, for your prayer is heard; and your wife Elizabeth will bear you a son, and you shall call his name John (Luke 1:9-13).

Zachariah couldn't believe what was being told and ask the angel, *"How shall I know this? For I am an old man, and my wife is well advanced in years."* Gabriel, in majestic humility answers Zachariah, *"I am Gabriel, who stands in the presence of God..."* (Luke.1:19).

I am Gabriel, who stands in the presence of God.

What an identity! He could have said, as many of us would be tempted to have done, "I am the mighty warring archangel who battles principalities and powers in the heavenlies." He could have said, "I am he who's eyes burn like fire and who moves at the speed of light through the galaxies." He could have said, "I am he who watched Lucifer get cast out of heaven with one-third of the angelic hosts." But his own sense of identity is found in living in the presence of God, the Throne room of heaven so he says, "I am he who stands in the presence of God." In this one sentence we get a fascinating insight into the thoughts of this heavenly being whom the Scripture records as performing two tasks only—warring against principalities and faithfully delivering the messages God gives for men. And we see in his words that he has no other desire but to stand in the presence of God in order to receive whatever instructions the Father has to give him. As Zechariah 4:6 says, *"not by might, not by power, but by the Spirit of the Lord."*

Gabriel understands firsthand what this means. Everything emanates from the infinite, overflowing, other-centered Triune God. All messages, gifts, powers, blessings,

"I am he who stands in the presence of God."

come from the presence of the Lord. This is the center of the universe, ground zero of all energy. Every good gift and the force of light and life itself flows from God. Where else would you want to be but in the presence of the Lord?

I want to live in such a way that these words could accurately be inscribed upon my tombstone. *"This man lived in the presence of God."* This is the secret of partnership with God. It is the culminating key, the crescendo of focus that puts you and me in a position to receive gifts from heaven to freely give them to those in need. This is the power of partnership that no extreme sport or thrill-seeking fantasy can deliver. And the wonderful news is that we don't have to stand outside the Temple courts while the priest offers incense. Now, by the offering of Jesus Himself, without spot, we are welcomed into the very Throne Room of God in the bosom of the Son, to stand night and day in the presence of the Lord.

If we were in a church service or in a classroom together right now, I would have you make this commitment to be one who stands in the presence of God. I would have you say it out loud— so why don't you read this out loud to the Lord and to yourself with a fresh commitment to the Lord:

My name is _____, I am he/she who stands in the presence of the Lord.

JOHN IN THE SPIRIT ON THE LORD'S DAY

The circumstances didn't look inviting for John. He had been banished to the Isle of Patmos in his old age. What had been a life of radical adventure probably now seemed to hit a dead-end. Remember, he was one of the "sons of thunder"—ready to call down fire from heaven. This is the same John who leaned on Jesus' chest at the Lord's supper, who had seen all the miracles Jesus did, and then outran Peter to the tomb to see that Jesus' body was no longer in the grave. This is the same John who was with Peter when he said to the lame man at the Gate Beautiful, "Silver and gold have I none, but such as I have I give to you."

By the way, the scene at the Gate Beautiful (Acts 3:1-8) is one of the clearest scenes of the spiritual gifts as compassion (i.e. the overflow of God's love). Peter and John didn't need a gift of healing for themselves. They needed it for someone else, and they received it so they could give it away. Notice the Scripture says this happened at 3 o'clock in the afternoon (the ninth hour), and it was on the way to the prayer meeting, not coming from it. It is a good prayer meeting when you come out of a time of passionate prayer so full that you raise someone out of their wheelchair. But this is better. These men have learned how to stay in the presence of God and by it, to stay full. They are distributing gifts of healing on the way to the prayer meeting!

Let's put this in perspective. Think about our normal rush to get the kids dressed, grab something to eat and hurry to church. Are we thinking about praying for someone in a wheelchair at IHOP? Could it be that this is how we should all live? Could it be that this is how we should come to church (or going anywhere else)—already full and passing out supernatural gifts from heaven. Perhaps we should at least be asking the Father for such adventures!

Decades later we find John on the Isle of Patmos physically, but "in the Spirit" spiritually. We all live a dual reality. At least to us it is a dual reality, which is a singular reality to God. By "in the Spirit" he means he is in the presence of the Lord in a unique way—we could say that he was more aware of the spiritual world than the physical one. In fact, he may not have been aware of the physical word at all. For John, on this Lord's Day, had practiced the presence of God in his life to the point that seeing into another world, while certainly unique in magnitude, was not unusual.

The Book of the Revelation of Jesus is a vision of all visions, yes. But in the sense of spiritual gifts it is the combination of two of the "revelation" gifts of 1 Corinthians 12; **the gift of the word of wisdom** (seeing part of God's plans and purposes for the future) and **discerning of spirits** (seeing the spirit world). John saw the spirit world of angels and the unfolding of God's cosmic purpose for earth and the heavens like no one else, with perhaps the exception of the Apostle Paul, who saw revelations that were not lawful to utter (2 Corinthians 12:4).

We could say, "Well, of course, he would see those things—after all, he is an apostle." But we don't get spiritual visions or revelations because we are in a position in the church or a position of spiritual authority. We see the things of God because we are hungry and thirsty for the presence of God and cultivate His presence. Jesus said, *"Blessed are they that are pure in heart* [single-eyed focus on intimacy with God] *for they shall see God"* (Matthew 5:8).

THE PRIORITY FOR THIS GENERATION

I have given you three significant stories underscoring the priority of God's presence. Samuel was raised in the presence of the Lord. Gabriel stands in the presence of the Lord, and John is in the Spirit on the Lord's Day. An objective survey of the Scriptures reveals the Bible is a compilation of stories of men and women who were hungry to know God, responding to the Father's heart to know and be known. Moses said, *"Show me your glory..."* (Exodus 33:18) and *"He that dwells in the secret place shall abide in the shadow of the Almighty"* (Psalm 91:1). David testified to the priority of the presence, *"I would rather be a doorkeeper in the house of my God..."* (Psalm 84:10) and *"How lovely is Your dwelling place"* (Psalm 84:1). Mary chose to sit in Jesus' presence and listen, and Jesus declared that Mary had *"chosen that good part, which will not be taken away from her"* (Luke 10:42). Anna, the prophetess, lived out her years in the Temple in fasting and prayer (Luke 2:37). The Church was birthed in an upper room of hungry and obedient saints who pressed into the presence of God for ten days (Acts 2:1-5). And millions of believers since then have chosen the presence of God over the passing fancies of this world.

I am so thankful I was raised as a child in two churches that put a priority on the manifest presence of God. I remember vividly as an elementary school child—arriving at church an hour early (every time the doors were opened) to go into the prayer room to pray. Then we would have "altar services" that typically lasted an hour or more after each service. I can honestly say I have been raised in the presence of the Lord. I was filled with the Spirit in that place of prayer at the age of nine. I was called into the ministry at the age of eleven (though I didn't really understand what that meant at the time—I just knew in my "knower"). As a teen we would meet at the church on Friday nights and passionately pray for an hour or two before going to "A Street Park" in Midland, Texas, and witness to the hippies, "goat-ropers" (cowboy wanna-be's) and anyone else who was there. I was "tattooed" in my spirit with the plans and purposes of God in those times of prayer. I learned to hear God's voice in those times of prayer, and I learned how to listen in the quietness as well. Fasting was not a strange thing to those of us who were hungry for God's presence. And my first experiences partnering with the Holy Spirit in the gifts—especially diversities of tongues and interpretation of tongues—came in those seasons of passionate prayer.

There are no shortcuts. The gifts of the Spirit are not the by-product of a formula of environmental or personality "keys;" but the result of a passionate pursuit by those that contend for the presence of God in their own lives at whatever expense of comforts or personal pleasure. And this generation will be no different. A generation that was raised receiving trophies for just showing up, I believe, will come to a place of holy dissatisfaction—to an awareness and longing that some things are worth laying one's life down for.

Today young people are giving themselves to radical Islam, many of them not really knowing what Islam is about. But they are hungry for meaning, for purpose, and to give themselves to something worth dying for. At the same time, this emerging generation is more sensitive to the needs of the world, to humanity's responsibility to steward global resources and the

The gifts of the Spirit are God's way to reach into people's brokenness and darkness with an overflowing supernatural supply. necessity to be a compassionate people to those who have been disenfranchised and marginalized by society. This generation of young Jesus-warriors is divinely prepared to take the Gifts of the Spirit as God's overflowing compassion in a way that my generation did not see.

The gifts of the Spirit are God's way to reach into people's brokenness and darkness with an overflowing supernatural supply. It is God's design to make the Church a global community of compassion, embracing and loving the marginalized as they are, not as they should be. The gifts of the Spirit were never intended to be squandered on the self-promoting, self-focused, or self-righteous spiritual orphans who are looking for a way to be validated by their own ministries.

Will you be one who will stir up the gifts? Will you be one who will seek out the presence of God at all costs? Will you be willing to fill your spirit with the Word of God, pray in the Spirit, get full and then give your fullness away? Are you one that would say with Gabriel, "I am he who stands in the presence of God"? The Spirit of God is sending out a holy "ping", a sonar sound heard only by the hungry and thirsty, but open for everyone. I believe the Holy Spirit is speaking to your heart right now—no matter what your age or background. Cultivate the gifts! And start by simply praying the following prayer.

Prayer:

Father God, thank You for giving me Jesus. Thank You for sending the Holy Spirit into my heart and filling me just as You promised. I want my life to count for eternity. I want You to use me—even though my mind would try to say it's arrogant to think You would want to use me. I want everything You have for me.

Father, I haven't been raised around a lot of people that know how to move in the gifts of the Spirit. But I want to learn. Teach me, Holy Spirit. Bring people into my path that know You better than I do, that can show me how to partner with You. Take all the events of my life—the good, the bad and ugly—and use them for Your glory. I want Your presence more than anything else. And I want others to know Your presence as well.

I commit myself to You, Father, in the name of Jesus and by the power of the Holy Spirit, who lives in me right now. Amen.

DISCUSSION QUESTIONS

1. What can we learn from Samuel's life about being committed to the presence of God?

2. What is the Bible probably not trying to say through Samuel's childhood?

3. Why should the Archangel Gabriel's sense of self-identity be significant to us?

4. What is significant for us about the Apostle John's being in the Spirit on the Lord's Day?

CHAPTER FOURTEEN

THAT MY HOUSE WOULD BE FILLED

"Trying to do the Lord's work in your own strength is the most confusing, exhausting, and tedious of all work. But when you are filled with the Holy Spirit, then the ministry of Jesus just flows out of you."
—Corrie Ten Boom

It seems appropriate to finish a book about God's gifts with the idea of a banquet. The gifts we have been talking about come from the God who beckons...

Come, everyone who thirsts,
  come to the waters;
and he who has no money,
  come, buy and eat!
Come, buy wine and milk
  without money and without price.
Why do you spend your money for that which is not bread,
  and your labor for that which does not satisfy?
Listen diligently to me, and eat what is good,
  and delight yourselves in rich food (Isaiah 55:1-2).

If you have been in church or have read through the Bible, you are familiar with the story Jesus told of the benevolent man who wanted to throw a great party for his friends, but they all had excuses to absent themselves. My hope is that you will see this story with new eyes to see God's great desire to give gifts to needy and broken people through a Church that is full and overflowing.

> There was once a man who threw a great dinner party and invited many. When it was time for dinner, he sent out his servant to the invited guests, saying, "Come on in; the food's on the table."
>
> Then they all began to beg off, one after another making excuses. The first said, "I bought a piece of property and need to look it over. Send my regrets." Another said, 'I just bought five teams of oxen, and I really need to check them out. Send my regrets."
>
> And yet another said, "I just got married and need to get home to my wife."
>
> The servant went back and told the master what had happened. He was outraged and told the servant, "Quickly, get out into the city streets and alleys. Collect all who look like they need a square meal, all the misfits and homeless and wretched you can lay your hands on, and bring them here."
>
> The servant reported back, "Master, I did what you commanded—and there's still room." The master said, "Then go to the country roads. Whoever you find, drag them in. I want my house full! Let me tell you, not one of those originally invited is going to get so much as a bite at my dinner party" (Luke 14:16-24, MSG).

Jesus doesn't explain why the invited guests were all giving excuses. Was there something about the host they didn't like? Was there some inter-personal strife going on between friends and no one wanted to be in the same room with each other? Were they tired of such banquets and taking the relationship with the host for granted? Jesus doesn't clarify, which means understanding those nuances isn't necessary in order to get the main point He wants to make. Jesus' main point about all of His parables is the Father's love and how the Kingdom of God is the way our life would be if we lived wholly in that love.

He sings and dances over us as an expression of His infinite love that cannot be contained (Zephaniah 3:17).

There are several points in this story I hope you will see that underscore what this book is about. The overview is that God wants to enjoy life with the friends He loves and He is sending out the Holy Spirit to invite them to come.

First, we see this is one of several stories where Jesus is describing God as a life-loving party-thrower. God evidently loves to have fun—and this alone is a major revelation for many people. Jesus is reinterpreting the Jews' misconceptions of God as a judgmental, law-giving, rule-keeping party-pooper to that of a totally complete, care-free God of joy and laughter. Do you remember the party the over-joyed father threw for his prodigal that had come home? And don't forget that Jesus' first miracle, the inauguration of his ministry, was at the wedding party. In fact, Jesus is telling this story at the dinner party of a Pharisee. God's universe is love-filled and overflowing. There is laughter in his courts: *"Then our mouth was filled with laughter, and our tongue with singing"* (Psalm 126:2). He sings and dances over us as an expression of His infinite love that cannot be contained (Zephaniah 3:17). Perhaps this view of a happy God would and should impact the way we actually serve Him!

Second, Jesus' story points to a table loaded with food. This is the picture of abundance, blessing and generosity. Again, Jesus is out to re-define religion's distorted image of God. On this table is everything we could dream of to satisfy the God-given desires—the many forms of human hunger. God is the source, everything else is resource. Why do we look anywhere else to be satisfied? What can we crave that God cannot righteously fulfill?

But the table represents more than food; it represents friendship, relationship, and for the Hebrew mind, the most important thing: shared life. While the Roman mindset declares "love is a decision," and the Greek mindset declares "love is a feeling," the ancient Hebrew world understood love as a shared life of togetherness—giving and receiving. This again points back to the Triune God, pouring Himself out, in infinite overflowing love, and in so doing filling the other members of the Trinity. *Fullness* and *being filled* is a huge concept in the Scriptures—especially the New Testament—captured in the dynamic of the word "fellowship" (*koinonia*). Have you noticed that God commissioned seven annual feasts, festivals, celebrations, or holy parties where His people were to come together and enjoy being together? It is captured in this story, but largely lost on the Western modern/post-modern mind.

What might be most surprising for some is to see that Jesus' metaphorical dinner host is deeply and emotionally attached to his desire to celebrate with his friends. When the servant (the type of the Holy Spirit who is going out and bidding guests to come and feast) reports to the host that they are all making excuses, the host is upset—in fact, outraged! Jesus' immediate meaning is not lost on His Pharisee audience; they understood Him as saying that the Jews had made excuses for why they would not attend God's party, so He was sending the Holy Spirit out to the Gentiles (i.e. "the misfits, homeless and wretched"). And, seeing that there is still room, the host sends the servant out to the outskirts of town! *"Whoever you find, drag them in. I want my house full! Let me tell you, not one of those originally invited is going to get so much as a bite at my dinner party"* (Luke 14:23-24, MSG).

Notice the consequences that come from the emotional investment of the host—"they won't get a bite." But don't mistake this emotional outburst as the will of the host. The host envisioned an evening of joy, laughter and fullness. That is His vision for the glorious event for which He has been gathering, planning, cooking and inviting. But his friends chose otherwise. Let me articulate it this way—we have mistaken God's fatherly tenacity to fill His house so we could enjoy Him forever, for a stinginess that says, "If you don't play by My rules you don't get anything."

But here is the point of Jesus' story and the heart of the Father reveals. It is "the punch line" if you will—"I want my house full!" Listen to the heart of the happy God saying, "I want my house full!" This is not to be confused with the American performance-driven idea of "packing the pew" or that someone's success or failure is measured by attendance or market share. This is an infinitely-overflowing God—living the can't-keep-it-to-myself-kind-of-love.

Nursing mothers understand the necessity of giving their breast milk to their babies and the physiological problems that develop if the feeding is overdue. Mothers will use the terminology of their milk "coming down," so that the feeding becomes rather urgent or mom is going to be in some pain. Now imagine, as feeble as this natural analogy is to the spiritual, that God's milk is always coming down; He longs to feed us. He called Himself *"El Shaddai,"* the Broad Provider, which literally means "the many-breasted one." You don't have to try to talk Him into blessing you. As Pastor Jack Hayford says, "Prayer is not about overcoming God's reluctance to bless us. Prayer is aligning ourselves with what God already wants to do."[12] It is simply believing and receiving—believing in who He is, believing that what He does is consistent with who He is, and receiving what He has for us. *"This is the **work** of God, that you **believe** in him whom he has sent"* (John 6:29).

Now let's look at the statement, "I want my house full" in two ways. I am not trying to play fast and loose with the text, but to hear it in the fullness of the Father's nature as *"El Shaddai."* We can hear the Father saying, "I want my house full. I want all my friends to come; I want every seat at every table occupied. Let's pack out the house." That would certainly be the plain meaning of the text in Luke 14. But knowing His nature—that He fills everything everywhere with Himself (Ephesians 1:23), hear Jesus also ascribing to the Father these words, "I want my house full. I want everyone who comes to eat until they are totally satisfied on my abundance; to come and dine until they are full!" Every mother understands that feeling. Every mother wants to spread the table at Thanksgiving with more than enough to fill everyone

The gifts of the Spirit are the constant "fount of blessing" flowing from an infinitely happy God...

in the house. And is God less gracious?

And why does God want us to be full? Because we cannot give what we do not possess, and we're not likely to give away what we don't possess in abundance. Again, *receiving* and *fullness* are important concepts in the New Testament and in the Kingdom. Remember, it's about compassion, not just power or possessions.

ARE WE STILL TALKING ABOUT THE GIFTS?

No doubt you have already made the connections and know where I am going with this story. How does Jesus' story of "the banquet spurned" of Luke 14 relate to the gifts of the Spirit?

First, the gifts of the Spirit were never intended to be a badge of accomplishment, a spiritual marker that says, "I get to sit at the head table because I have a gift." Gifts are not a mark of spiritual superiority. Nor are gifts of the Spirit a First-century Church "booster rocket" just to help the early church get launched off the pad, then that booster falls off into history's ocean. The gifts of the Spirit are not a mechanical decision God makes every few hundred years in Church history to help boost the Church through a tough spot. Nor are the gifts to be consumed by those who are to be carriers of the gift—like gluttonous waiters gorging themselves just behind the kitchen doors on the meals they are supposed to be serving to the hungry guests!

The gifts of the Spirit are the constant "fount of blessing" flowing from an infinitely happy God through a Church that is being daily overloaded with one grace after another (John 1:16).

JUST NOT EXCITED ABOUT GOING

But what the story also says is that there are those who have lost the joy of the invitation. Perhaps there was a time when the invitation to attend a special banquet and to be fed and filled with the most exquisite fare was all a person could talk about, but now it has lost its sizzle. Perhaps some of the earlier attendees became the object of harassment or resentment because they had attended the special event and others didn't; had stories to tell that others did not have. Now, it is just easier to say, *"I have taken a new wife and need to spend time with her,"* or *"I have bought some oxen and must prove them"* (Luke 14:19-20).

God is Still Beckoning

I believe the Holy Spirit, the great servant of the Father's house, is moving throughout the earth again -- to the "misfits, the homeless and the wretched." The Holy Spirit is being sent to the highways and the roads less travelled to reach a new generation that will not consume the gifts upon themselves, but see themselves as carriers of the presence and gifts of God.

There is a new generation that wants to see all mankind as equals, just as God made them to be; to take people at face value and accept them as they are, not as they should be. To live without labels and without walls. It is the joy of the Father's heart to send out an army of people who simply love people and want to connect. But Jesus' last words to His disciples are relevant for the new generation as well, whether it's a spiritual generation or a demographics generation, *"Do not depart from Jerusalem, but to wait for the Promise of the Father . . . and you will receive power and you shall be witnesses to Me..."* (Acts 1:4, 8).

A great social gospel of passivity and appeasement won't cast out the devils and heal the cancers that are real and destroying the people we seek to help. Along with Christ's condensed version of the commands, *"Love God with all your heart, soul, mind... and love your neighbor..."* (Luke 10:27), He also said through the Apostle Paul, *"Be filled with the Spirit"* (Ephesians 5:18), and *"desire the best gifts"* (1 Corinthians 12:31; 14:1). It is the operation of the supernatural gifts of the Spirit that break into people's private world and gets the message home, "God loves· you with a never-ending love, just as you are, not as you should be. But he loves you too much to leave you as you are."

It can't be said better than Paul said it, inspired by the Spirit, *"May the love of God, the grace of the Lord Jesus and the fellowship of the Holy Spirit be with you"* (2 Corinthians 13:14) as you get full and then joyfully give yourself away, only to discover that, in His fullness, you never have less, but more, after you have given yourself away.

DISCUSSION QUESTIONS

1. In the story of the Great Banquet who is Jesus trying to describe to His listeners?

2. Why do you think Jesus felt this parable was so important?

3. What does this story tell us about the Abba of Jesus?

4. What does this story tells us about the gifts of the Spirit?

APPENDICES

NEW GENERATION QUESTIONS

Luke 12:54-56 speaks of understanding the signs of the times. Jesus seemed genuinely amazed that His followers could be so expert in the things of this world but couldn't see the things of the Spirit. In my concern for a new generation's lack of exposure to the gifts of the Spirit, I asked a group of twenty-somethings for some questions that they have (or know that their contemporaries have) related to the gifts of the Spirit. These are not the only questions, nor the only answers—perhaps not even the best answers. But these are real questions from a new generation. My hope is that these may stir a dialogue and a hunger for more of God in our daily lives.

I grew up in church and my life is fine without the Holy Spirit. So what's the point?

That would be a good question to ask the Lord—and then get quiet and listen for a while. I would suggest you say, "Lord, your cousin John (the Baptist) announced that You would baptize with the Holy Spirit and fire. What did he mean and why is that important? Lord, why did You tell Your disciples to go wait in Jerusalem until they were filled with the Holy Spirit, when You had already breathed upon them to receive the Spirit? What was the point, Lord? Is there something I'm missing?" I'm confident that if you ask the Lord sincerely, and listen, He will begin to talk to you about "the point."

Many would answer with a series of questions, "What is your definition of life?" What do we mean when we say "life is fine"? Do we mean life is free of major problems? Do we mean we have a regular income therefore we can take care of whatever needs might arise? Do we mean that we are on our way to the American dream and don't want anything to disturb our progress?

I would also answer that question asking different ones; for example, are you living with the understanding that your purpose is to re-present Jesus in His current glory as savior, healer, and baptizer? Are you living to impact others with the resurrection life of Jesus? Have you ever experienced someone getting healed as a result of your prayer? Do you live out of such overflow fullness that you are giving away your money, your time and your knowledge to others to the point of adventure? Can you say you are living the competition of generosity? Have you experienced what it's like to know that the more you give yourself away, the more you realize you don't have less than before, but more?

There is no question that God has given every believer a "well of salvation" that leads to eternal life (John 4:14 KJV), but He also offers to turn that **well** into **rivers** of utterance, revelation and power, by a baptism in the Holy Spirit (John 7:37-39). What's the difference between a well and rivers? Movement. Dynamic power. Potential for major change. He has given us the Holy Spirit in overflow measure because we have a job to do that requires power. Your well of salvation will get you to heaven, but rivers of living water will enable you to take others with you, and bring some of heaven to you. It's about bearing much fruit and that our fruit should remain. My prayer is that a new generation can redefine "life" for a generation that is not sure if life is worth living.

How does the Holy Spirit affect my everyday life? Why is it important? Is it important?

I hear a lot of younger believers asking this question, "Why is it important?" It leads me to understand that there is a generation in the Church that has not yet been exposed to the real deal— and thus my motivation for writing this book. You don't miss what you haven't experienced. Those who have been raised in the church's youth group in the last twenty years have probably been more exposed to foosball and pizza than to the power of God and the life of the Spirit. Some of that is a leadership issue, not a youth issue. We thought the things of the Spirit were too deep for young people and talking about spiritual things would drive them away. In reality, there is a generation coming on the scene that is very vulnerable, susceptible to radical Islam or anything else that looks like it will make them a hero or call for their total sacrifice. Only the Holy Spirit will turn you from a zero to a hero. If you hang out with the Holy Spirit He'll make you look like a genius. If you hang out with Holy Spirit He'll fill in the holes in your soul and produce a security that makes you look more cool than James Dean, Paul Newman, Bono and Matthew McConaughey all rolled up into one (you may have to Google some of those). He made you. He knows what you were born to be—and trying to be anyone else makes you look needy and phony. Somebody said, "You make an incredible you, but a lousy somebody else." And Holy Spirit is the only one that makes you the real you.

When we look at the life of Jesus we find a young man who was totally committed to doing life with the Holy Spirit. He didn't do anything without the strength, direction and courage of the Holy Spirit (Acts 10:38). What we have tried to instill in this book is that we can cultivate a life in the Spirit that enables every believer to do the same works Jesus did—and in the sense that there are now millions of believers on the planet—greater works than He did.

If we're doing so well (as Church) without the gifts of the Spirit, then why do we need them? It seems they were good for another time and place.

Jesus said many things that seem good for another time and place, unless we understand that God's world is an eternity that encompasses all He has made in the visible world and the invisible, time and eternity. You and I were made for another time and place as well. But our view is very narrow (especially when we are younger). Have you heard about people getting older and "facing their mortality?" That means that there comes a point in time for most of us when we have more time behind us than we have ahead of us. Perhaps we've lived 60 years and, barring tragedy or illness, we may have twenty or thirty years left. We begin to see things differently, time is shorter, and how we spend it takes on new significance. We start living smarter, not harder. Stay with me.

Now think about Jesus, who coming from eternity into time realized early-on how significant each short day really is. (James said our whole life is like a vapor—a wisp of smoke in the air). So with this eternal perspective, Jesus says something very difficult for a new generation to grasp, *"The man who loves his life will lose it, while the man who hates his life in this world will keep it for eternal life"* (John 12:25).

What? I'm supposed to hate my life? We are taught just the opposite; life is about living it to the fullest, a selfie-worthy life, building memories and loving life. But compared to what is in-store (and at stake) for eternity, this life means very little except for making an eternal impact. The only thing we can take with us is the souls of men. True riches, as far as God is concerned, is the souls of men, not rewarding experiences and great friends, though these have human value (Luke 16:10-11). This sounds harsh, even blatantly wrong to our self-centered, time-bounded ears.

Now we can deal with the question: "If we're doing so well (as Church) without the gifts of the Spirit, why do we need them..."

It should be stated plainly that we are not doing well as Church without the gifts of the Spirit. If we are measuring success by gathering crowds in a few places for a one-to-two hour gathering once per week, we're not even doing that well. In fact, we have been steadily losing market share (percentage of those we are responsible to reach) for the past 50 years. That alone should alarm the Church. Each year we are closing down as many churches as we are opening—a few churches are growing, but largely at the expense of other churches that are shrinking. But the mission is not filling up a few buildings on a weekend. The mission is to make disciples of the nations—to preach this good news that the Kingdom of God has come in power (and is within reach to everyone), and to preach it to every people group!

Said another way, we seem to be leaning our ladder against the wrong wall. The goal is not to gather a few folks and try to keep them all safe within our building, but to get them full of heaven's compassion and send them out with heaven's power. And the reason we're not sending more out in heaven's compassionate power is because we have marginalized the work of the Holy Spirit when we come together. The goal of the Church has never been to help people find a happier here and now, to learn to cope with their problems or just find a comfortable group, though these are great by-products of Kingdom wholeness. The goal from day one has been to get people so full of heaven itself that we can't help but give it away. This is what Acts 2 and "stay in Jerusalem until you are filled" is all about. And this means a discovery that this life is to be "hated" in comparison to the life to come. The only way the Church will fulfill her mission is by the power of the Holy Spirit—and one of the primary ways Holy Spirit gives us enough of heaven to give away is through the supernatural enablements—that is, His manifestation gifts.

Why would I want the Spirit in my life when I've seen so many weird pastors or moments in the church with "the Spirit" at the center?

Allow me to look at the question as it is stated. I know I only polled Christian young people for these questions, but this doesn't sound like it is coming from a Christian. "Why would I want the Spirit in my life...?" Of course we would know that you can't be a Christian just by praying a prayer to some invisible someone and getting mysteriously stamped for the next train to heaven. You have to be born again, and to be born again, Jesus said, is to be born of the Spirit. You can't be a Christian without having the Holy Spirit indwell you.

But beside a bizarre notion that one could be a Christian without the Holy Spirit, what is interesting to note in this question is that the presence of the Holy Spirit is associated with weirdness; weird pastors or weird moments. I understand the notion that people have done strange things in the name of the Holy Spirit. I just wonder if we would have considered Jesus' ministry too weird to take seriously as well. Spitting on a man's tongue, for instance, or making a mud salve with spit and dirt to put on a man's eyes might not have seemed as strange in Jesus' day (we rationalize), but even then raising the dead could not have been understood as common.

Under what circumstances, then, would we see miracles and healings as acceptably "not-weird"? Can we only accept healings now if they have been duly processed by the medical community that, by the way, largely does not believe in healing and miracles as a work of God? Or are we willing to accept "moves of God" as long as they are conducted in a stoic and clinical way? And who gets to decide what is weird and what is not? I find people that do most anything different than me are "weird." I'll even say it to myself out loud, "That's weird." I find lots of new fashion statements as weird, and I used to think that a fried egg on a hamburger was weird, until I ate one. When I went to the former Soviet Union I saw men kissing men on the cheek— that was weird. And in Africa, men hold hands while walking down the street—not a sign of homosexuality but heterosexual friendship—but I said, "that's weird." The point is, it was weird to me but not to them because of the cultural differences; weird is relative.

Ultimately, only God gets to decide what is weird. And I choose to let Him use me any way He wants—and if He gives me the choice (which He usually does) I can obey Him in non-weird ways. But ask Ezekiel if laying on his left side for 390 days, then on his right side was weird (Ezekiel 4). He would probably say, "It was worse than that! But it was God." Let's not be too quick to judge. If we are hungry enough, our definitions of "weird" become more flexible, and perhaps that's more of a lordship issue, after all.

Can we have all of the gifts or are we limited to one?

To answer this question clearly and carefully, a distinction must be made between the **Father's gifts** (motivational gifts, Romans 12), the **Son's gifts** (ministry/leadership gifts to the

Church, Ephesians 4:11-12), and the **Spirit's gifts** (manifestations as the Spirit wills for the common good, 1 Corinthians 12). This is an important distinction because most of the "gifts assessments" available today lump all the gifts into one bucket, without distinction, and imply all the gifts are the permanent possession of each believer. The Father's gifts can be described as the possession of the believer because they are "hardwired" into every human person in his mother's womb. The Son's gifts are permanent in that they come through callings to serve as an equipping leader and these gifts and callings are irrevocable (Romans 11:29). So we can say, "I have such and such gift" and "I have such and such calling." But the manifestation gifts are different in that they come and go as occasion and need demand. We may all pray to be used to distribute the best gift for each occasion. Paul tells the Corinthians, *"All these (manifestation gifts) are empowered by one and the same Spirit, who apportions to each one individually* (severally [KJV]) *as he wills"* (1 Corinthians 12:11), and *"Earnestly desire the best gifts..."* (1 Corinthians 12:31).

Now, with a clear understanding of the distinction between those gifts that are the permanent possession of the believer and those that are temporary and occasional manifestations, we can say any believer who is willing to cultivate a partnership with the Holy Spirit in boldness and submissive obedience, can be used to distribute any of the manifestation gifts of the Spirit (1 Corinthians 12) as the Spirit sees fit. Yes, it requires faith and partnership on the part of the believer being used of God, but this is true of anything we do to fulfill our commission and calling in the kingdom. We should all covet, earnestly desire to be carriers and distributors of the overflow of God's compassion at the point of people's needs.

Remember that the gifts are not the possession of the believer through whom they are delivered. They are given, as the Spirit wills (1 Corinthians 12:11), for the benefit of those needing the gifts. If you had a gift of prophecy, you would be able to prophesy at will. But it doesn't work that way. The Holy Spirit is the giver of the gift, and He delivers it to the person needing prophecy through anyone who is willing to partner with Him in the process. So, if we make ourselves available to partner with the Holy Spirit, He can deliver any of the gifts through us, as the need demands. Paul says for us to "covet the best gifts." What are the best gifts? The ones that meet the need. If a person is sick, he doesn't need a word of prophecy as much as a gift of healing. But if he is making a critical decision, a word of wisdom may be better than working of miracles.

I have prayed for people to be healed and they are not. What happened to the "gift" of healing there?

Remember, the gifts of the Spirit are as the Spirit wills, not as I will, though I have a responsibility for how to administer His gifts to others in appropriate ways. This is not to say God wills for some to be sick and some to be healed. No, He paid the same price for every person's healing as He did for every person's salvation (Isaiah 53:3-5). The good news is that there are numerous ways people can receive healing—the manifestation "gifts of healing" are just one way. He has commanded us "to lay hands on the sick and they shall recover" (Mark 16:18), to call for the elders of the church (James 5:14-15), to pray the prayer of faith (Mark 11:24), to believe/receive the healing word when spoken (Matthew 8:16), to only name a few. Every time I pray for the sick it doesn't mean I am operating in a gift of healing. It simply means I am obeying what Jesus commanded me to do. In those cases, my faith and the person's faith that I am praying for has a role to play, and God decides how and when the healing will come. But when the manifestation gift of "gifts of healing" is in operation there is little faith necessary for the sick person needing healing; it is a free gift from God as an overflow of God's compassion—from the Father, through Jesus, by the Spirit.

There is always the question, why didn't they all get healed? It's a large topic, and many have addressed it. Suffice it here to say, we live in the in-between age of the Kingdom of God— in the now-but-not-yet. The Kingdom has come (inaugurated in the resurrection of Christ and outpouring of the Spirit as down-payment), but it has not fully come in consummation (sin, sickness, brokenness forever banished). In this in-between age, we still see through a glass darkly and don't operate with perfection. But we have enough of heaven to give away to prove heaven is real and to make men thirsty for more. It is important to leave the "whys" to God and get on with the "who" and "how"— who needs what I have and how do I get it to them in the way they can receive it.

When I was seventeen, in the summer between my junior and senior year of high school, I travelled with a singing group called The Living Letters. It was an amazing experience for a kid from Midland, Texas, to travel from Dallas to Des Moines, to San Francisco, then through Los Angeles, back through Albuquerque, to Jacksonville, and back to Dallas again. We finished the tour leading the worship for the Full Gospel Businessmen's International annual conference at the Statler Hilton with Kathryn Kuhlman and Jerry B. Walker as the keynote ministers. I was fairly cynical of goofy stuff being passed off as supernatural ministry at the age of seventeen. I was all about authenticity. Then I began to see people come off of hospital gurneys, out of wheel chairs, throw down crutches and take back braces off. I thought I had been around a lot of healings and gifts of the Spirit until I saw healings and miracles like I had never seen before. I became hungry to partner with God in whatever ways He wanted to use me.

A short time later Kathryn Kuhlman was a guest on the Johnny Carson Show, (what is now the Late Show or Late Night with Conan O'Brian, etc.). I was not normally allowed to watch late-night television, but to see this miracle-working evangelist on The Late Show was unique and I was intrigued. Johnny Carson asked her why so many people who received healings in her meetings end up sick again. It was intended as a "gotcha" question but I will never forget her answer. She said:

"These are gifts from God and don't require any faith on the part of the people. It's my faith and my prayer that makes those gifts available to them. But because they haven't developed their own faith to receive healing, many don't have the faith to keep their healing either, and about eighty percent will lose their healing within six months."

I don't know if Johnny Carson was still listening, but I was.

Gifts of healing are different from the prayer of faith, healing by the laying on of hands, or by believing what the Word of God says about healing in the atonement. Gifts of healing are just that—free gifts—and we cannot claim to know exactly how or to whom the Holy Spirit will give these gifts. Our objective is not to understand it all and have answers for every question, but to be available and willing.

How come it seems that more healing/miracles/gifts happen in other countries?

I have a theory that has been derived from years of observation concerning faith. My observation is that we have the most difficulty believing God in the area of our expertise. Where we feel like we have humanly acquired knowledge we don't see the need for God's help. Peter and some of the disciples were "professional" fishermen; they didn't want to take directions from a rabbi about which side of the boat to cast their nets. They were the experts. Pharisees didn't want to hear Jesus re-interpret the Scriptures for them. They were the experts. The orators on Mars Hill (Athens) didn't want to hear the Apostle Paul—"Who is this babbler and what's this business about a resurrection?" They had studied Plato, Socrates and Aristotle.

In the West, we've become too smart for God. We know how the germs work and what prescriptions will deal with which illness. Our first response tends to be toward natural and medical remedies rather than to God. It is difficult to have simple faith about things with which we have gone to great lengths to fill our heads with human education. We have the most difficulty believing God in the area of our expertise. This is not to say there is a premium on ignorance over education—but a premium on heart knowledge over "head" knowledge. Both have their place.

When I minister in developing nations where there is a lot of poverty and fewer medical resources, the people don't have the same hurdles. They don't have access to the same resources and need God to heal them. Miracles and healings are relatively easy in those scenarios. Where those same under-developed peoples have a Catholic background it is even more so; they believe in

God and in Jesus as Son of God, but have usually never seen Him do what they have heard He does. So when you tell them "He is here to heal you," they line up.

When ministering in the island of Samar, Philippines, the crowds filled the downtown square as far as the eye could see. There were reportedly 50,000 there and listening on radio. We preached a simple gospel of the compassion of God expressed through Jesus Christ. We gave an invitation for people who wanted to be healed each night, and each night the line for prayer extended out into the darkness. Every time someone would testify over the speaker system that they had been healed, the line would grow longer. By the end of the week our team had received a lawsuit filed by the doctors and pharmacists of that area because they had no business that week. The people simply believed God, and God gave them gifts.

Again, I am not suggesting that we should prefer ignorance over education. I am saying we must teach educated and sophisticated people the difference between primary knowledge (spiritual knowledge) and secondary knowledge (natural human knowledge; cognitive "head" knowledge). We must teach believers the difference between the "knower" (man's spirit) and the "thinker" (man's mind). God is a spirit (John 4:24), His words are spirit and life (John 6:33), and we can only know Him in our spirits (1 Corinthians 2:4-14).

What percentage do you think is genuine when it comes to healings?

The short answer is, I believe all healing is genuine. If people get healed as a result, the healing is genuine—whether it is by a spoken word, hands laid on the sick in prayer, mud clay on the eyes, dipping seven times in a dirty river, medical prescriptions or the natural recuperating process of the human physiology. All of these come from God.

But I suspect this student was intending to ask about healing ministries in the church, and in particular so-called faith healers. The skepticism or even possible cynicism seeps through in this question. Can you hear it? I actually appreciate it. I was there as a young person. I appreciate the premium on authenticity and the question that seeks an answer.

Think about this: This youngest generation has enjoyed from birth technological advances no other generation has had. The disadvantage that comes with it is being raised as "marketing targets." Young people know that every person and voice coming to them via technology is playing an angle; a hidden agenda. This generation has endured more commercials than any previous to them. This is why the new cultural generation places such premium on authenticity, and is equally suspicious. It is also why they now value immediate relationships, the fathers and mothers, over every other relationship. Surveys tell us that even if their parents are scoundrels or delinquents, these young people look to them as most influential in their life. What does this say about how we are to be reaching this generation?

Answering an earlier question I mentioned how Kathryn Kuhlman, a great miracle and healing evangelist, publically stated that only 20% of the people that received healing in her meetings actually stayed healed. And her reasoning was on the basis of a lack of maturity in faith to be able to contend against the enemy for the healings they had received. Jesus tells about how the birds of the air come immediately to steal away what was sown in the heart (Mark 4). So to ask, how much healing is genuine means we must understand all the ways healing comes. It means we must understand that God can even use someone who is not perfect—perhaps not even serving God. He used Balaam to prophesy blessing over Israel (Numbers 22:38; 31:16; 2 Peter 2:15). He moved upon two men to prophesy that failed to show up to Moses' meeting (Numbers 11:27-28). He used King Cyrus, a Gentile leader, to serve His purpose for rebuilding Jerusalem (Ezra 6:3) and prophesied through a corrupt high priest named Caiaphas at Jesus' own trial (John 11:51). If I am hungry for God I won't care if He has to speak to me through a donkey, and I might even hear Him speak to me in church!

It is our misplaced priorities of being "right" over being rightly-related and relationally whole that has set us up for such judgmental thinking. It sets us up to ask such questions about "how many are genuinely healed." I hope you have caught my heart in these pages—that if you are ministering to people out of the overflow compassion of God, even if you miss it—or even if someone else isn't doing it just right, God is at work. If we are ministering to people because we want what is best for them as an overflow of God's love in us, we won't be so concerned about such questions. This is not to say that one can be sloppy in their personal life or character and still fare well. Sooner or later, it catches up to the casual seeker, the corner-cutter and the con artist. But don't let those keep you from following hard after God, and staying full of God, and giving all of God away that you can give. Be a God-partner, not the spiritual police.

Do you remember when Peter asked Jesus about what would become of John? Jesus said, "What is that to you?" (John 21:21-22) In other words, there's no profit in concerning yourself with how God completes His work in other believers' lives. God is "able to make them stand and keep them from falling" (Jude 24).

How do I know what manifestations of the gifts are genuine and others are not?

Here is the word "genuine" again in the question. John addresses this point bluntly to believers, "Try the spirits to see whether they be of God" (1 John 4:1). And Paul says that "I make known to you that no one speaking by the Spirit of God calls Jesus accursed, and no one can say that Jesus is Lord except by the Holy Spirit" (1 Corinthians 12:3). A good test for the manifestations is to see whether they point to Jesus as Lord and draw people to the heart of the Father. Even if they may seem "weird" to us, we must know that Holy Spirit is more interested in people being reconciled to God than we are.

Many have heard a "doom and gloom" or judgmental prophetic word. Why would God say that?

I have briefly addressed the difference between inspirational and revelational prophecy in a previous chapter. All believers can prophesy as long as it ministers edification, exhortation and comfort (1 Corinthians 14:3). Those who stand in the leadership office of the prophet may be used of God to speak to nations, cities, churches in ways that minister correction, but for the most part, the ministry of prophecy in the New Testament is very different from that of the Old Testament. Jesus has taken the judgment upon Himself at the cross and is ministering compassion through His Church. Even when there may be an element of caution or correction, the person prophesying is responsible to deliver that in a way that builds up, encourages, and comforts.

If you have heard a doom and gloom judgmental prophetic word, I am sorry. You were subjected to those who weren't taught well. They were probably doing what they heard someone else do and thought that's what prophecy is supposed to be. Sometimes we hear bad preachers; they are not trained well and take Scripture out of context. But we don't deduce by the poor caliber preaching that all preaching is illegitimate. Nor should we deduce that because we heard someone misuse the gifts, that they are illegitimate. Sometimes they are simply not trained well or have had poor role models.

Do I have to hear God before operating in the gifts? Does it have to be a Holy Spirit prompting? What does that prompting feel like?

I don't have the whole answer on this question because I only know how the Holy Spirit has used me. He undoubtedly works in different people different ways (diversities of gifts, administrations and operations—1 Corinthians 12:4-6). If we understand the manifestation gifts as partnership in ministry with Holy Spirit, then we would assume there will be some understanding on the part of the carrier that he/she is giving a gift to someone.

For me this often comes by the gift of a word of knowledge. The Spirit prompts me that someone has a particular need and I am to help get the answer to them. At times, in the church, I have either had a "knowing" that the Lord wants to heal a certain ailment, or I have even had the symptom of that in my own body. Initially that was very confusing to me because I would have some pain or sensation I had never had before, and, since I've rarely ever been ill, this was confusing to my mind. Then I came to understand through intercessory prayer that these empathic symptoms were one of the ways the Holy Spirit "clues me in" on what He's wanting to do. I'm actually feeling what someone else in the congregation is feeling. As a pastor, I would call that ailment out (as best as I could describe it), and ask those who are experiencing that ailment to receive the gift the Lord has for them. I have found that speaking out or announcing the gift the Lord is offering causes faith to rise in people's hearts. It is as though Jesus were in the room saying, "I'm here; what would you have me do for you?" (Mark 10:51).

At other times I would know in my "knower" (my spirit) before a church service began what would happen in that service. Jesus said the Holy Spirit would lead and guide us into all truth and show us things to come (John 16:13). Sometimes this includes "the news before it happens." I learned as a pastor to spend time praying in Spirit the evening before a service, or the early morning hours of a service, and on occasion the Holy Spirit would show me what was going to happen in that service. Sometimes it would be a different way to conclude the service than I had planned, sometimes it included certain needs he wanted to minister to in that service.

My wife and I were ministering in San Juan, Argentina, one summer and had taken an all-night bus trip from Buenos Aires to San Juan, only arriving in town an hour before the Sunday morning service with just enough time to take a shower, dress and get to the church. There had been a crying baby on the bus, so sleep was sporadic. I was tired and asked the Lord to give me supernatural strength and refreshing for these hungry people. When we arrived at the church I found a quiet room and prayed in the Spirit for a few minutes and got quiet on the inside. Then the Holy Spirit said, "This is going to be easy." And when He spoke that word I saw the service that was about to happen. I saw myself preaching, and while I was preaching people would receive a gift of healing and would just stand up. I saw people popping up and down like popcorn all over that auditorium— not as the result of an altar call, but just receiving gifts from the Lord and standing up and giving thanks for it. With that word in my spirit came an instant refreshing. I knew that I knew this was going to be easy (from a natural stand point). I joined my wife on the front row as the worship was already in progress. As we were introduced to the congregation (it was our first time in that church), I simply told the congregation what I saw. Then I began to preach and people began to receive healings all over the auditorium throughout that whole message. And, yes, it was easy. It was one of the easiest days of ministry I have ever had—the Spirit of God was strong in my weakness. His yoke is easy. There is no struggle in the Spirit.

We left that service and ministered in two other cities before coming back to the same church the following Wednesday night. Do you think people showed up for the Wednesday night service? Absolutely. Because of the free ministry of the Spirit the previous weekend, the church was packed with people standing in the lobby and outside the doors throughout the meeting. Where the Spirit is Lord (allowed to do what He wants) there is liberty (2 Corinthians 3:17).

How much does my personal sin/life hinder the gifts?

In my humanness I wish I could say that God won't use you unless you are walking "the straight and narrow." It would be easier for all of us to discern the good apples from the bad apples in ministry if the gifts and callings of God were immediately revoked when someone falls into sin. But the reality is, God is not as judgmental as we are. No, He doesn't bless a sinful life and yes, we will give an account for every deed done in the body (Matthew 12:36). But God's compassion for those needing His gifts is greater than His discomfort in delivering those gifts through imperfect vessels. And as I have stated in an earlier question, He uses very imperfect people (e.g. Balaam, Cyrus, David, Solomon, Peter, Paul, etc.).

There are some famous (or infamous) examples of ministers who were powerfully used of God to minister healing and deliverance to thousands of people, who bought into a deception that because God still used them when they had messed up, that somehow He was giving them special permissions or license.

This is the oldest deception Satan has—"Look how long you have been serving God, and look at how He is using you! You deserve a little special treatment."

Two things every believer needs to be aware of in partnering with the Spirit in ministry: 1.) When you are tired physically and mentally you are more susceptible to temptation, and 2.) Moving in the things of God exposes you to some pretty powerful feelings; in fact, power and adulation can be addicting. Samson was deceived by the power of God in the sense that he began to believe that he would always have the power of God no matter what. The Spirit of the Lord still came on him to do the miraculous, even though he knew he was trespassing his Nazarite vows. But he misunderstood the Spirit's tenacity to act in behalf of God's people for a condoning of his own actions. Some of the most tragic words in the Scripture are about Samson, *"For he did not realize that the Spirit of God had departed from him"* (Judges 16:20).

In some ways, the Spirit of the Lord will minister through us in spite of us. And that can be deceptive. In other ways, we can get so busy doing the work of the Lord that we lose connection with the Lord of the work, and we begin to ignore His voice. His voice becomes more and more faint, and we actually become susceptible to familiar spirits—we want/need to hear spiritual direction so badly (or we want a word of knowledge because people come to expect it of us) that we are willing to listen to other voices. The only answer is humility, brokenness and constant dependence upon the Lord—which should be walked out and worked out in daily time spent with Him. Yes, our personal life can have direct impact, for good or evil on the operation of the gifts of the Spirit in our lives.

What can we do about the gifts of the Spirit if my church publicly or covertly renounces it?

Change doesn't work very well from the bottom up. If you have a hunger and desire for the gifts of the Spirit to move in your life but your church doesn't support and teach the ministry of the Jesus by the overflow gifts of God, then there are three basic options (others may be available in unique situations).

First, go to your pastors and let them know you are interested in being used of God in this way, and ask for their suggestions and guidance. This is to humble yourself as one who honors leadership and it can also be a way God uses to speaks to leaders.

Second, ask the Lord to use you in personal ways to bless people without fanfare or publicity, being mindful that to give prophetic words requires spiritual overseers to judge those words. Operations of the gifts need accountability, but not platform or notoriety.

Finally, you may need to find a church that supports, teaches and encourages the operation of the gifts of the Spirit so that you can grow and flourish under proper supervision. But whatever you do, don't assume that God is using you to bring a change of direction or understanding to your church if you are not in leadership in the church. The ultimate outcome will be discord and division, and that never works out well. God is not the author of confusion.

Isn't it true that God is more concerned with our character than our gifting or charisma?

There is a popular notion that has been perpetuated through the years, and it "preaches well"—that character or charisma is an either-or proposition. In fact, it is a fundamentally flawed question because character is not something we can engineer for ourselves, it is the result of the indwelling work of the Spirit, or else it is not the fruit of the Spirit. The fact is, both the gifts of the Spirit and the fruit of the Spirit come from the same place— they are the work of the Spirit in our lives and only a mechanical worldview suggests that one is more important than the other, especially when we understand the gifts of the Spirit are an overflow of God's unchanging, other-centered nature of love and compassion.

Well-meaning leaders want Christians to grow in their spiritual maturity. Every pastor wants every member of the flock to be strong in the character of Christ, transformed into His image to the degree that godly decisions are made; loving God and others is a priority over loving self. But often the way this priority of Christian virtue and ethic is promoted is by contrasting character over and against gifting. It is often shaped up in a question like this: "Would you rather have the character of Christ or the gifts of the Spirit?" Sometimes it is stated as, "Would you rather have the fruit of the Spirit or the gifts of the Spirit? The question sounds cogent and pithy. Most believers have heard all their Christian life that both of these, Christian character (the fruit of the Spirit) and the gifts of the Spirit, are things to be valued. So, why do we have to make them an either/or proposition? Character and gifts are never an either/or proposition, but a both/and opportunity.

Why would I have to choose one or the other? If gifts are an overflow of God's infinite, unchanging, other-centered nature of love and compassion, then why would I have to do without one or the other? The reality is that both gifts and character—the gifts of the Spirit and the fruit of the Spirit—are an overflow, a by-product of the work of the Spirit in a person's life. Both come from the Holy Spirit and are a result of fullness in God that allows us to become conduits of His love, forgiveness and blessing.

Why do we make it an either/or proposition? One reason we position these two works of the Spirit against each other is because we don't actually view the fruit of the Spirit as something the Spirit does within us, but something we do in response to the commands of Christ. We have made the Christian life a Roman-esque "quality decision" rather than an overflow fullness of the Person of Jesus who is *"the fullness of the godhead bodily."* Paul's prayers speak of a desire for believers to *"walk worthy of the Lord, fully pleasing Him, being fruitful in every good work"* (Colossians 1:10). So that sounds like something I must choose to do: make good quality decisions to do the right thing and don't do the wrong things.

What we fail to see in the equation is that Paul prefaces the "do" with a "be." Just prior to his prayer statement that the believers at Colossae would conduct themselves in a worthy manner, he prays that they would be filled (Greek: *Pleroma*—full to a point of continual and ceaseless overflow) with the knowledge of God's will. For Paul, **being** always precedes **doing**. I like to say, "who you be" comes before "what you do" (an intentional abuse of the grammar).

Frankly, another reason character and gifts are presented as antagonistic to one another is that many have only heard the "horror stories" of faith-healers and charlatans that abuse the body of Christ. If our only concept of the gifts of the Spirit is in the context of self-promoting abusers, then one can see why it would be easy to contrast that against character. But there is neither need nor advantage to position the two against one another, as though one was more important or more spiritual than another.

In the beer commercial "the most interesting man in the world" says, "Stay thirsty, my friend." In other words, keep reaching for more experiences of adventure, because this present life is all we've got. But I say, "Stay full, my friend." Love God, love one another and stay full to the point of constant overflow—of both of the gifts and character of Christ. Because you and I are drinking from Him, the Source of something that will last forever—and there's enough to give away—and still have no less than you did before you gave it.

SUGGESTED READING

Baker, Heidi. *Birthing the Miraculous: The Power of Personal Encounters with God to Change Your Life.* Lake Mary, FL: Charisma House, 2014.

Bell, James S. and Stephen R. Clark. *Christian Miracles: Amazing Stories of God's Helping Hand.* Avon, MA: F+W Publishing, 2005.

Bennett, Dennis and Rita. *The Holy Spirit and You.* Alachua, FL: Bridge-Logos, 1998.

Bonkke, Reinhard. *Taking Action: Receiving and Operating in the Gifts and Power of the Holy Spirit.* Charisma House: Lake Mary, FL. 2012.

Clark, Randy. *The Essential Guide to the Power of the Holy Spirit: God's Miraculous Gifts at Work Today.* Shippensburg, PA: Destiny Image, 2015.

Cook, Graham. *Developing your Prophetic Gifting.* Grand Rapids: Chosen Books, 2003.

Drain, Wayne and Tom Lane. *He Still Speaks: Embracing the Prophetic Today.* Southlake, TX: Gateway Create, 2012.

Hayford, Jack. *The Beauty of Spiritual Language.* Nashville: Thomas Nelson, 1996.

_____. *The Finger of God.* DVD. www.jackhayford.org.

Hayford, Jack, ed. *The The Hayford Bible Handbook.* Nashville: Thomas Nelson, 1995.

Hagin, Kenneth E. *The Holy Spirit and His Gifts Study Course.* Tulsa, OK: Rhema Bible Church, 1991.

_____ *The Gifts of the Spirit: Unlocking the Mystery of Spiritual Gifts.* Tulsa, OK: Rhema Bible Church, 2013.

Horton, Harold. *The Gifts of the Spirit*. The Revival Library: www. revival-library.org, public domain.

Ireland, David. *Activating the Gifts of the Spirit*. Kensington, PA: Whitaker House, 1997.

Keener, Craig S. *Gift and Giver: The Holy Spirit for Today*. Grand Rapids: Baker Book House. 2001.

Liardon, Roberts, ed. *Smith Wigglesworth: The Complete Collection of His Life and Teaching*. Tulsa: Albury Publishing, 1996.

_____. *Smith Wigglesworth on the Power of Scripture*. New Kensington, PA: Whitaker house, 1998.

_____, Compiled by Copeland Ministries. *John G. Lake: His Life, His Sermons, His Boldness of Faith*. Ft Worth: Kenneth Copeland Ministries, 1994.

McNutt, Francis. *The Power to Heal*. Notre Dame: Ave Maria Press, 1997.

_____. Healing. Notre Dame: Ave Maria Press, 1994.

Prince, Derek. *Gifts of the Spirit: Understanding and Receiving God's Supernatural Power for Your Life*. Kensington, PA: Whitaker House, 2007.

Sanford, Agnes. *The Healing Gifts of the Spirit*. New York: HarperCollins Publishers, 1966.

Sumrall, Lester. *The Gifts and Ministries of the Holy Spirit*. Kensington, PA: Whitaker House, 2005.

ENDNOTES

[1] Are we satisfied with measuring nickels, noses and numbers? Have we given up on making disciples because we feel that spiritual transformation can't be measured? In my last senior pastorate I developed what I called the "Kingdom Business Report," which was a box in the corner of the Sunday bulleting where each member of the church could document how many people they ministered to during the week—salvations, healings, personal ministry, etc. If the business adage is true that "we get what we measure" I wanted to measure the right things. It was an attempt to measure transformation and ministry by those I was charged to equip. There are ways to help people become more aware of their ministry partnership for their 9 to 5 world.

[2] The letter in its original form can be found at http://www.theologyinworship.com/2015/05/13/dear-church-an-open-letter-from-one-of-those-millennials-you-cant-figure-out/#more-1050.

[3] Jean Darnall, "The Ministry of the Kingdom of God." Lecture presented in the Ministry of Healing modular class, Van Nuys, California, February 27, 2008. The King's Seminary, Van Nuys, CA.

[4] Roberts Liardon, ed. Smith Wigglesworth: *The Complete Collection of His Life and Teaching.* Tulsa: Albury Publishing, 1996. p.815-816.

[5] Carroll Thompson has been a professor at Christ for the Nations Institute (Dallas, TX) for over 35 years. He wrote several courses, including, "Possess the Land," that deals with spiritual warfare and deliverance. http://www.carrollthompson.org/.

[6] *Southern Baptist lift ban on speaking in tongues*—June 2015. http://www.joy105.com/southern-baptist-convention-lifts-ban-on-speaking-in-tongues/.

[7] Pastor Robert Morris used this title for his book on the Baptism in the Holy Spirit.

[8] Spiritual language is an experience as by-product of Spirit baptism; though it is often called "the gift of tongues" which adds to the confusion between glossolalia as manifestation gifts (which is "as the Spirit wills") and glossolalia as personal prayer language (as the believer wills).

[9]For more on the benefits of spiritual language order the teaching series "The Beauty and Benefits of Spiritual Language" Passages Bookstore, Gateway Church, Southlake, TX., www.gatewaypeople.com.

[10]Order the CD series entitled "Bringing Your Devotions to Life." www. DrKerryWood.com.

[11]See Leonard Sweet's, *SoulTsunami: Sink or Swim in the New Millennium Culture.* 1999.

[12]I have sat under Pastor Jack Hayford's teaching ministry for more than thirty years. This quote, attributed to Martin Luther, may be in Hayford's groundbreaking book, "Prayer is Invading the Impossible." Luther said, "Prayer is not overcoming God's reluctance. It is laying hold of His willingness."

ABOUT THE AUTHOR

Kerry Wood is passionate about authentic Christianity lived in the power of the Spirit. In over thirty-five years of pastoral ministry he has focused on the local church, prayer movements, and community transformation initiatives. He has launched or sponsored several church plants in the U.S. and abroad and has spoken in leadership conferences, crusades, and local churches in more than twenty countries and throughout the U.S. He has authored a variety of ministry materials, published articles, Bible curricula- and audio-video teaching.

As a local church leader, seminary professor and member of the Society of Pentecostal Studies, Kerry is committed to partnership with Holy Spirit, intercessory prayer, teaching the Word, five-fold equipping of the Church, leadership development and church planting. He endeavors to steward partnership with the Holy Spirit through the gifts, and introducing people to Spirit Baptism. His philosophy of life and ministry is about 'being' before 'doing', an overflow of God's fullness as the source of all activity.

Kerry holds a Doctor of Ministry and Master of Divinity from The King's University (Los Angeles), a Masters of Arts in Biblical Literature from the Assemblies of God Theological Seminary, and Bachelors in Christian Ministry from Southwestern Assemblies of God University.

Kerry is married to (Dr.) Ana (Chiqui) Wood, and has four grown children, Robert, Geoffrey, Audrea, and Lauren.

www.DrKerryWood.com

www.TableofFriends.com

Made in the USA
Lexington, KY
29 April 2018